Russia Ukraine War

Origin Of The Conflict, Its Effects On The Global Economy Till Recent Military Mobilization By Russia

(Factual And Summarised Insight Into The Ukraine - Russia War)

Daniel Kenny

Published By **Bella Frost**

Daniel Kenny

All Rights Reserved

Russia Ukraine War: Origin Of The Conflict, Its Effects On The Global Economy Till Recent Military Mobilization By Russia (Factual And Summarised Insight Into The Ukraine - Russia War)

ISBN 978-1-77485-889-9

No part of this guidebook shall be reproduced in any form without permission in writing from the publisher except in the case of brief quotations embodied in critical articles or reviews.

Legal & Disclaimer

The information contained in this ebook is not designed to replace or take the place of any form of medicine or professional medical advice. The information in this ebook has been provided for educational & entertainment purposes only.

The information contained in this book has been compiled from sources deemed reliable, and it is accurate to the best of the Author's knowledge; however, the Author cannot guarantee its accuracy and validity and cannot be held liable for any errors or omissions. Changes are periodically made to this book. You must consult your doctor or get professional medical advice before using any of the suggested remedies, techniques, or information in this book.

Upon using the information contained in this book, you agree to hold harmless the Author from and against any damages, costs, and expenses, including any legal fees potentially resulting from the application of any of the information provided by this guide. This disclaimer applies to any damages or injury caused by the use and application, whether directly or indirectly, of any advice or information presented, whether for breach of contract, tort, negligence, personal injury, criminal intent, or under any other cause of action.

You agree to accept all risks of using the information presented inside this book. You need to consult a professional medical practitioner in order to ensure you are both able and healthy enough to participate in this program.

TABLE OF CONTENTS

Introduction 1

Chapter 1: Ukraine's Genius 4

Chapter 2: Unavoidable Russia And Ukraine Conflict From A Neutral Observer 15

Chapter 3: Encroaching Neutrality Could Threaten Credibility 21

Chapter 4: Real Reason For The War Let's Put An End To The Blame On Putin The Reason For This War Was Practically Unavoidable 28

Chapter 5: Inspirations From China 45

Chapter 6: The Fears In This War Rationality Vs. Phobia 52

Chapter 7: Russia As A Global Player 58

Chapter 8: The Reasons Is There A War? 78

Chapter 9: Understanding Vladimir's Putin 136

Chapter 10: Conflicts Impacts On Economies 175

Conclusion 183

Introduction

The human race had eliminated polio black death and smallpox but we were unable to eradicate the most brutal killers of our time. There was nothing that killed more people during history than human-made conflicts. Since Mankind did not have into a world where war was no longer the primary method of settling disputes, it is an adolescent part of human society.

We had sent people to space with the hope that one day intelligent aliens would appear however, we did not have the thinking to believe that in the present time and in this age humans still viewed conflict as an essential means to deal with differences.

This Russian and Ukraine conflict is yet another example of the deficiency in the human race, regardless of the fancy words It demonstrates that we are able to think like angels even when the gun isn't directed at our heads, or our future seems to be slowed or uncertain. The reason we think that peace and harmony should be the norm for our society is because we did not think of any existential threat. Come out of it, we are human beings and our brutality has helped us survive, so it is safe to say that war is part of our lives. As long as humankind exists and is a part of it, war is necessary but at the same time, Ukraine and Russia are being sucked into a bloody, inevitable war, because in their own books there is an absolute reason and necessity for war in particular because both sides saw certain actions of the other as a threat to their existence.

You must be able to comprehend the motives and real reasons to this conflict by looking in a critical manner, free of bias and illusions created by the Western as well as Russian propaganda media. This conflict is not only all about Ukraine or Russia but almost the entire globe.

In the event that this war is in full swing, most of the population is on the cloud. Others are simply watching the war on TV or in the major newspapers which you may get the information they want you to look at or read with independent sources such as the internet, where you will are able to see the latest footage of the sufferings and the blazing chaotic events in the midst, but these bits of information are often presented in ways that alter our judgements. However, in the real world there's the little boy from Ukraine crying and asking Mummy what's happening? What is the reason they are bombing? The world is far more unaware of the facts than the young boy, because both parties that are in charge of the decision-making aspect of the war feed the world deceit and propaganda. If you want to know the real reason of this conflict, this book has been made available for this exact goal.

Chapter 1: Ukraine's genius

Ukraine has succeeded in portraying herself as the one who was the victim of the war Maybe they they're not, however the nifty actions of Ukraine have made all of the world overlook that this is not an unconventional conflict among two nations.

Ukraine isn't as shocked as they portray in this situation. At the very least they were prepared for it prior to 2014 when the annexed of Crimea by Russia was a sign of an invasion threat. Ukraine was getting ready and knew that they would battle Russia in the future.

The Silence treatment that upset Russia

After the annexation Crimea, Russia got a somewhat chilly response from Ukraine. Still, silence was gold; the silence shook Russia which led Russia to continue to harass Ukraine. Russia was suspicious and looked for an answer in various ways. However, the silence of Ukraine was getting unbearable and at the same time, Ukraine sorted to join NATO as a way to consolidate Ukraine in the event of the possibility of a showdown with Russia.

Russia knew that Ukraine's decision to be a part of NATO was an attempt to do something huge and they responded with an invasion. For Russia the annexation to Crimea was an explicit slap on Ukraine's face. Russia was awareof it, so that it appeared as if you had slapped someone, and they were in silence, while going about gathering allies and perhaps weapons, you'd be worried as you are aware that the punishment could be cooling down and is on the way.

Ukraine Did What They Wanted

The approach of Ukraine was so clever that it's going to take an examination of the facts to see the harm they've caused to Russia. It's true that Ukraine was not able to join NATO and I'm not able to tell whether she really would have liked to join NATO at all, however, she now has the favorable support of NATO as well as NATO and the European Union. The two member states of the union were previously Russia's main partners in numerous important fields.

Prior to this, aside from the normal tense relationship in the relations between United

States and Russia, Russia was among the most friendly nations in the world working alongside the other nations in areas of research and development agreements, energy and space exploration. Today, Russia had lost at most 50% of those amazing possibilities.

Ukraine realized that Russia was more connected than she was and then sought to isolate Russia from the world and then fight Russia one-on-one in a manner that appeared to be conventional. The idea of Ukraine was so clever that the world didn't just discredit Russia but instead embraced Ukraine.

Ukraine was able to blow this conflict out of proportion even giving it a global War III coloration; at the same time, it could be a regular war between two countries The inroads made by Ukraine's silence increased the severity of the conflict into one of global scope in terms of implication, concern and impact.

Ukraine was just trying to defeat Russia and ensure that Russia isn't able to utilize her global connections. However, Ukraine was so good that they're now fighting Russia through Russia's global network and Russia is on its own in a way, creating a equilibrium.

The Cold War Between the United States (NATO) and Russia as the basis that prompted Russia's incursion into Ukraine.

The War is rooted in the Cold War era. Ukraine is an unfortunate victim that was caught between two giants, both considering the strategically important location of Ukraine extremely valuable. More than any other country in which United States and Russia had ever reached a conflicting desire. Ukraine is perhaps the most significant in the entire period that was a part of the cold war which saw several presidents leave and come back throughout both the United States and unions dissolved in the former USSR, Ukraine seems to be the final battleground of the cold war. Everybody wants to achieve victory over Ukraine by the use of force or goodwill. But this is a problem in the face of each Russia as well as the United States disregarding the independent fate of Ukraine.

The conflict has been fought one between NATO as well as Russia; Ukraine is only used as a battlefield. Ukraine is facing the shot, but maybe not to benefit either NATO or Russia however, if it is able to achieve the rightful and legitimate autonomy from both giants. we aren't sure what this will mean for Ukraine but only the time will determine...

Putin is exploiting Putin's Omniscience Syndrome of the United States and the Pack Psychology of NATO

It is believed that the All-knowing Complex of America is used by Putin and he's employing America United States in a special method to try out the waters. The issue with the American omniscience condition is that they wish they could know everything. They think they are omniscient and are always able convince everyone that they know everything; Putin recognized this characteristic that is characteristic of United States.

When this omniscience-based complex is paired with NATO's psychological pack, you've got Putin playing around with the world. The issue in NATO is the way they act as an animal pack; when one person goes, other members follow, without asking any further questions.

It's quite amazing that United States intelligence is almost always able to anticipate Putin with a high degree of accuracy, this should not be a surprise to anyone, Putin is actively playing his friends in the United States his cards, at first he tries to muddy the waters and observes reactions. He is aware that the eyes of the world are focused at America and, as a way of ensuring not to enter into any conflict against America, Putin takes care not to enthral America. United States. Russia as well as America are the best of partners in ways aren't always understood by us. Both countries respect each one another.

American intelligence is the one intelligence agency to know Putin's plans for invasion, and then began an evacuation process for Americans to Ukraine; Putin delayed the invasion for a week to allow America to evacuate its citizens. Putin is studying American body language United States and acting in the same way, according to indications. Putin is able of expressing his wishes towards America. United States, and he is smart enough in making appear like an intelligent break, but the majority of these are just Putin's various ways of observing what America will react when he makes his actions.

We're looking at Putin as a person who has a omniscient psychology. He would like America to become the only one who knows everything. He would like America to seek out the thoughts of Putin is thinking and what Putin is planning to do next. After he has taken America into this all-knowing, complex, he gives them the next one; and then he pauses to analyze the strategy America uses to counter the situation. He realizes it is it is because the United States is the leader of the NATO packs, and the chief of the West as well and that they all act according to the psychology of the pack as if they are wolves, and once they cross the path, the rest follows . Putin is in control of all of us by letting his United States predict his moves and exploiting the all-knowing system in The United States as he wages the War in Ukraine.

If anyone is Omniscience In this instance the case is Putin because he knows what people are thinking. Everyone is trying to determine what's going on inside Putin's head; this means that Putin realizes that everybody thinks about him. we believe Putin is a tough guy. Putin has a reputation for being a hard man, Putin knows that we believe that he's the toughest person since Putin believes that he's an extremely tough person, and almost everybody can anticipate Putin and that's the reason Putin knows what people are thinking.

My Observation is as neutral as I wish it to be, may appear pro-Russian since this war is focused on Russia, Ukraine may appear to be fighting the conflict, but what I see is a furious determination of a people who want to take control over their fate in an era where the need of a human being is more important than human rights. I sincerely would like to wish the Ukrainians Ukraine the best, however, should they not find an area to call their own the time is now to accept their place. No one is able to stop Putin in the event that when he stops his march and it will get to Ukraine before it reaches this point.

NATO as well as The World Also Played into the Hands of Ukraine This Should be Ukraine in addition to Russian War Not World War III It's not the case with a NATO war.

We have been entangled in, perhaps not knowing that this is a Ukraine as well as Russian war, not a war between the worlds and it is still the battle between two sovereign nations , and so long as one of them have not crossed their border of invasion intentionally or in any other way the war remains the war of two countries.

The conflict remains mostly traditional, and we be aware that Ukraine was at least anticipating the war from 2014 following the annexed of Crimea but I am proud of Ukraine for not letting its guard down for so long in a truly strategic decision, regardless of the way we view it, Ukraine had done well in gaining global sympathy and an impressive amount of support.

There is a common belief that NATO or it's United States led Ukraine into the war, but it's the other way the other way around. It was Ukraine that sought out NATO or even European Union and not NATO trying to contact Ukraine and begging for her to join NATO so it was Ukraine who brought NATO into the war, not NATO deceiving Ukraine into a war of fate.

It is crucial to ensure that the war gets the attention it is due. Ukraine was doing fairly well. What Ukraine requires most is the international attention this situation is receiving; this has placed her in a distinct position from the incursions from Syria, Libya, etc.

Ukraine has cleverly transformed the war she was fighting into something exciting, and even turned it up as a potential element for a World War III. Do you think this war is more important than any of the other wars of the last fifty years? I would like to congratulate Ukraine for transform this conflict into one that kept the entire the world in awe. This isn't happening simply because it's Russia it's happening because it's Ukraine who came up with a method to have the entire world engaged in their fight and that's a feat of genius.

Chapter 2: unavoidable Russia and Ukraine Conflict from a neutral observer

The most striking Western propaganda about the present Russian and Ukraine war is that the war could have been avoided, the fact that Vladimir Putin alone is responsible for the war and that Putin has opted for war over diplomacy it is true that there has been war, there was a cold wars, and so propaganda is not without its place, but regardless of how easy it might appear for people to blame Putin and, honestly, if one party was to shoulder the most responsibility for this war, it would take the blame from Putin and Russia but if we look at the situation from a different perspective we might see that the war isn't so unavoidable as some of us seem to make it appear.

The war was always going to occur and it was just simply a matter of timing and now is the perfect time to see it happen The reality lies that our world could become more militarized in the future as the world becomes more technologically advanced, there will always be dangerous military escapades that do not respect territorial integrity. This is the moment that has the largest population of people in the world, and tomorrow , there will have more people. the current 1% would be lower than 1% by the time it happens. we can eliminate 1% today , if we can fix it the future, that's Putin's mindset and I'm not sure I think I've ever seen a more exceptional humanist. We believe that wars are expensive today, but they will be even more costly in the future and if the war were to happen then let it be today.

If we consider this, we can see it is true that Russia is pushing its propaganda. Western media has blocked out the majority of Russian media outlets, but right from the beginning, Putin made it clear that he doesn't care about whether the entire World particularly those in the West as well as NATO considers him, so blocking blocking Russian propaganda from the West doesn't alter the fact that at home Russia's propaganda department is advancing all the time. Russian propagandists are pushing all of the arguments for the Ukrainian invasion, and is receiving the support of the majority or at the very least, popular support.

The most interesting aspect is that, despite the numerous messages that both factions are trying accomplish is to keep their base loyal. In fact, the conflict doesn't require any more pressure to justify the necessity, but the war that is not supported and backed by loyalty will be lost regardless of how legitimate or important the motive for war it is essential to keep supporters to remain committed. The best method of doing this is with the traditional propaganda.

The truth is that the war cannot be avoided but convincing people that this war will not be avoided is to make it appear that it could be avoided if the other side took specific steps. Those weren't the main issue. It's an attempt to manipulate the general public's perceptions that don't reflect the reality The truth is that both sides are trying to promote the myths that this war is not a problem until a certain point that, for example, in Russia the story may be telling us that the war could have been avoided until Ukraine brought in enemies within the

Russian borders , while Ukraine as well as Western allies are feeding us stories that the war was able to be prevented through diplomacy before Russia entered Ukraine and invaded Ukraine. All these stories are merely fabricated to keep the blinds on but the reality is that if you believe it or not, the build-up of tension was too long and the conflict's bone too fragile, and If we had pushed the issue to the extreme then eventually there could have been chaos.

Putin is considering the future, and not only his own future, but also the potential future for the Russian Federation; we need to know a few things. Russia is the largest country in the world in terms of area and also the most rich country in terms of mineral resources, the management of such a vast expanse requires a robust approach, and democratic values or western values can't be implemented in Russia in the way that we might like to imagine There are risks of a revolt when the more liberal values of democracy are permitted to penetrate into Russia and regions in Russia being aware of how rich they can be should Russia fell apart, it's quite tempting for members of the region to seek an independent status from Russia or even rebel in the event that the country isn't in the grip of an apparent communist government, in this instance it is possible to imagine the possibility of civil war within Russia in the event that Russia decide to not do anything now.

For the part of Ukraine it is important to contemplate the reasons for the reason why this conflict is inevitable. There is a real desire for complete independence and sovereignty. Ukraine would like to become sovereign within the true sense, to be a part of her destiny and become an eminent and respected member of the international community. It's not an unreasonable request, however this dream is not in line with Russia's existence for the event that Ukraine is a officially USSR country decides to withdraw from the USSR and stand alone as a amazing democracy, and be doing it excellent, it would be a threat to Russia's futuristic company existence.

Ukraine isn't the only nation to break out from the old USSR however Ukraine is, by far, the most important, second only to

Russia itself. I don't think it is possible to cause a revolution throughout Russia since they might be enticed by the prospect of shedding their dictatorial regime for democratic rule, in which the situation could get out of control and the country could collapse. Ukraine could also be at risk of civil conflict in the event that Russia persists in its interference in the internal matters of Ukraine I'm hoping that we now understand why the conflict isn't difficult to avoid as both sides make it appear.

Chapter 3: Encroaching Neutrality could threaten credibility

It was evident that in the cases that of Russia and Ukraine neutrality becomes extremely difficult to sustain and when you consider countries that have had a history of neutrality, such as Switzerland abandoning it and then what is the real issue.

The location between those in the West along with the remainder of the world is quite predictable. For those who appear to be more of a mystery or a hidden, it's an open secret. Nearly all people in the world was a bit aloof from the nations of Africa. Africa.

The world's leaders have never sought to be right. They were looking to be strong perhaps because the strong always are right. In this case it is not a good idea to dwell on the morality of the war will just create a burden people in the world don't actually need if we seek the truth. For any nation or an individual to be so angry to be willing to wage war it is essential that the stakes be important.

We in Africa have escaped this war, not because of weakness, but because we seem weak, we're weak, however we stayed out of the war since there was nothing to gain from it and my impression is of total neutrality and a lack of apparent silence on this continent in Africa.

In every war in which the winner was always shared the stories typically more elaborate and thrilling stories, which appear more reliable, but regardless of the moment in conflict, the tales of either side will not be accurate enough; However, the impartial observer that is expected to present the most truthful story would be skewed by lack of contact, but an impartial observer is most likely to relay the story which is at the very least trustworthy.

We are currently engaged in the midst of war, therefore we're not writing story, we're watching it unfold and at the conclusion of the day the winner will create the proper story, or we could be in a state of balance and each block would be able to tell their own stories to their viewers.

A war that is not truly neutral is devoid of truth in the midst of the conflict in the background, we all are watching from the script provided for us by actors who decide what they want us look at, regardless of the side you are on and you'd been reading about a variety of flimsy information, you'd seen an entire fable.

I'm not convinced that I'm competent enough to address this issue and not because I lack expertise of military strategy or the world's politics, but simply because I'm from a Third World country (Nigeria specifically) which we had consciously chosen to stay out of this war but we were fighting our own wars when the world opted to remain neutral by telling stories, and selling weapons until we saw the situation in a collective obligation of the international community.

In this situation, without real neutrality or credibility in the supposed second and first world nations I'd need to come in and give my perspective Although it might not be as interesting, but it is at least important that somewhere, in some way, someone is trying to discover the truth about the situation.

It is possible to have an even more convincing report from Ukraine herself, perhaps in a scenario where Russia was fighting another nation, Ukraine had stayed neutral for a significant portion of her sovereign rights and in this particular instance, Ukraine herself had been attacked, which had revealed an emerging trend that led formally neutral countries like Switzerland to abandon her neutrality. The premise in this case is that neutrality will not protect you from invasion as the other nations had opted to defend their own parts. China as well as North Korea may be a bit silent, but they take an opinion, China has been the most silent, due to her economy and debt towards the United States, the Middle East countries have always been divided between those who tolerate for Israel and the United States and those that do not conceal their hatred, in this case it's easy to determine which countries fall on the middle of the division, India as well is taking a very predictable position with respect toward Russia particularly amid the ill-fated sanctions.

We don't have much faith in the truth from the West particularly from NATO and the other allies outside of the western part of the USA as well as anything of a reliable source or reliable from Russia as well as her allies.

The United Nations seems biased, it's a war between two sovereign states, but it seems that the United Nations is concerned about moral implications and focusing on "who has invaded the other" in lieu of "why the war" but I wouldn't bet on that the United Nations to act anywhere differently. The majority of VETO nations are NATO members, and China is not going to be in the middle of two giants, however the United Nations, in this case, is an ineffective bulldog which is most important in the field of humanitarian concern . Currently, it's not as if the two conflicting factions have any concern about UN guidelines, Russia has the ability and even declared that it would not obey UN as NATO is calling the shots in UN; NATO is in an icy war with Russia, United

Nations is not much of a factor in this situation in the event that we consider United Nations as factions where there are NATO, Russia and China and, of the course China can be considered to be in a class of its own.

We in Nigeria we have become massively aware of the fact that we are neutral in this situation since if the conflict was purely one between Russia and Ukraine we would naturally choose Russia's sideand not try to analyze the morality of the issue we have more history of ties with Russia than we do with Ukraine as a nation that has had more trade agreements with Russia than we've been able to do with Ukraine that could make it easy for Nigeria to get the backing of Russia If the war was solely in the conflict between Russia or Ukraine and it did not seem as if Russia was aggressive, however there are other legitimate issues.

Nigeria is most likely to be in the interests of the West since we gained an independence form Britain and have a very strong relations with both the United States and the European union nations, it might be considered normal sense to set up our tent alongside them but this isn't the case, UK, US, European Union are not yet in war, or even in war, the second issue is what's involved in the battle for us? What do we gain by taking sides and, in all honesty, I'm aware that our position in the global arena is among the least valued, but in light of the fact that we must be able to appreciate ourselves enough to not create chaos that has the potential of further causing instability in Africa in the midst of countless instances of poverty, corruption disease, hunger and many other human-made and natural vices that have afflicted the African continent. Regardless of how much our opinions may not count as Africans in general , and Nigerians specifically, we remain out of the political situation, and we are in a better position to present the facts without prejudgment.

Chapter 4: Real reason for The War Let's put an end to the blame on Putin The reason for this War was practically unavoidable

The expansion of Western values across Russian borders is something that would be looked at, but it's not the reason to change your mind and cause harm to your fellow brother; I prefer to refer to the term "going astray" to describe Ukraine from Russia's point of view, Ukraine is going off course We must be objective in this situation, Russia believes that Ukraine is going off course and it could be. However, Russia don't understand that Ukraine differs from Russia and that the values that might be beneficial for Ukraine might not work for Russia In reality the people evaluate a country based on what they have learned about their own country, but the reality is that what works for one country might not be applicable to the other as what people think of as Russia that kept it in place was its communist-like ideology, whereas the one was what held the majority of Western nations together was their democratic system.

The issue is, can the true democratic values and western values work in Ukraine? Yes, it could but what implications do they have for Russia and a possible desire for values based on Ukrainian culture that would not be beneficial for Russia ultimately, Russia would implode and be in the middle of chaos.

What implications do these have for Ukraine? Following Russian rules will result in Ukraine could be an appendage to Russia which would severely limit the sovereignty of the state. Even if we would like to claim that diplomacy would solve this issue in the end, this war was inevitable, it was bound be a reality someday, whether Russia allows Ukraine be free to do what it wants and then fight to stop the uprisings within Russia and fight back to bring Ukraine on the right track, the most important thing to remember is that with the democratic system and Western values serving Ukraine and Russia was under constant sanctions that affected her economy, in the long run, Ukraine would be way better off than Russia and this could create an impression among the people of Russia that the country's system was ineffective or its leaders failed, and a revolution for change would be the best option, particularly the citizens of Russia that they are able to observe the false benefits from Western principles in their neighbor (Ukraine).

We must be able to shield ourselves from sentiments and emotions, this war is perfectly justified for both sides, Russia is not going to let an ally of the enemy penetrate its borders and people in the future. the same however, Ukraine also is not ready to surrender its independence to become a part of the world community to achieve Russia's imperial objectives and objectives. In this scenario, it doesn't matter who was first to attack the two sides have real need for war, and I'm glad that they are fighting now and not in the future. both countries are at risk of a conflict in the coming years should they not fight each other.

I'm not sure which is more costly: an unending civil war between one of the two countries , or an armed conflict between the two nations; but it's more beneficial to have fighting between two countries rather than a civil war either of them, which is why I hope that the current conflict doesn't cause the outbreak of a civil war between either of the two nations, as there are a lot of chances for both Russia or Ukraine being exploding inside, and this moment could be the most likely to cause Russia to explode within , however in the event that the two countries stay intact, then this conflict is the least expensive option.

From on the Side of Ukraine This war is crucial

It might seem like an over-the-top panic in Ukraine This war is a source of lots of anxiety and a large amount of determination. However the anxiety that comes with living in Russia is a real concern in the minds of Ukrainians and what's the purpose of living in Russia and what is the reason for this fear.

The war is more important to Ukraine more than any other nation; it is a war of fate, Ukraine couldn't have rejected the war and continued to be sovereign, it's a major aspect for Ukraine and, from a the perspective of Ukraine it is impossible to have rejected the war, unless they want to be loyal or a part of to Russia The danger of being subordinate to Russia can be a risk because Ukraine isn't Russia in the sense that Russia will always be first, regardless of what the goal of Ukraine is, it doesn't matter so long as it is in opposition to the interests in Russia, Ukraine would be the perfect instance of contemporary subjugation.

Russia will never be able to provide for Ukraine greater than Ukraine will take care of itself therefore, being under Russian rule is highly resented for the Ukrainian population. Both parties perceive an existence-threatening threat to the situation, Ukraine believes living under Russia is a threat to its existence while at the same time, Russia considers a free Ukraine as a threat to its existence.

The answer lies in your views and the perspective of whose do you see yourself

In every other conflict, our emotions are being played with; where you receive your information will determine your view of the events. The majority of sides would claim that they don't want to fight, but looking at the concern of both sides would provide us gain a more realistic understanding how you view Putin as a monster or as a person fighting for the sake of the future of his country and its stability. country will depend on the location and how you're evaluating and processing the data.

When we look at the information in Western press, we might observe a monster in Russia If we read the details about the war in Russian sources, it is possible that we can observe Putin as well as Russia seeking to rescue Ukraine as well as Russia from the severe repercussions of the future However, when we obtain information from sources such as the internet, we could be able to see a hero like Zelensky and an entire epitomize of national pride and courage within the Ukrainian population. Ukraine but we still see an immense amount of confusion and suffering and are unable to figure out the right decision. this level of suffering on an people that just a two years ago lived in an entire country. The third category of people are the real issue of Putin those who are unable to comprehend the situation since this is the group which Putin is concerned about, whether you're Russian or Ukrainian or anywhere else in the globe, and belong to the category that is able to see suffering, confusion and a touch of Ukrainian bravery, then choose to get closer to the traditional Western and Russian media.

This is talking about the future, or the next generations. The main cause of the war is the influence of values that resulted in the loss of Russian traditional values. Imperialism is not a popular choice however the idea the idea that Ukraine will take on Western principles is considered a major crime in the eyes of Russia. Russian Federation; these are the things we should know, Russia sees Ukraine as an ally and maybe someday Russia would fall in love with Ukraine. Ukraine might be able to take over in the road to a better future while still maintaining regional values. In one sense, Russia clearly understands how difficult it is for the head that is crowned and Russia does not see itself as we see her currently in the near future.

It is the norm in Super Powerful countries to groom successors, especially when there is a clear possibility of losing influence, and typically, grooming a nation with similar values is the most effective way to remain relevant, even if you have long outlived your significance. The United Kingdom did it by grooming a variety of countries, such as those of the United States and Canada, in the present, it is the UK can be more powerful than other nations that have similar status. Russia wanted to groom Ukraine but should that fail to work, then it is time to assume control of Ukraine or sabotage her.

Russia recognizes its potential in Ukraine and doesn't wish to see her achieve its heights through untrue connections. Ukraine has the same potential as Russia However, Ukraine doesn't have Russia's fights. Ukraine could excel without fighting the wars that Russia has been fighting for a long time, Ukraine can go far in truth, Russia would like to become Ukraine's forever benefactor, but the manner in which it's coming is becoming a bit foreign for Ukraine and that's a risk and in the future, everything Russian might be unrecognizable to Russians which is the primary issue.

There were significant changes in the region from Russian perspective the anomaly must be rectified. However, even in the event that Russia was successful in Ukraine but the more significant risk is the fate of Russia itself, Russia was at every angle, Ukraine is the final frontier and, if Ukraine is lost, Russia herself could be in danger before she gives up and it might not take that long and that is the main reason behind the conflict.

A war Between Brothers is the Worst Kind of War

Maybe we view Ukraine from the perspective of the former USSR or from in the context of regions like Eastern Europe or through the perspective of a shared border. regardless of how we see the issue, Ukraine and Russia had been living for a long time together that it is fair to call them brothers.

Vladimir Putin had never hidden his conviction of the fact that Russia or Ukraine are sister states. the majority of these assertions would be confirmed by ancestral connections. Russia isn't the gloomy beast that people are painting however Ukraine does not require an overly smug and insecure big brother.

In the view of Russia, Ukraine is going off the rails, but in the mind of Ukraine, Russia is taking away the freedom of Ukraine. The best way I could explain the situation between Ukraine along with Russia is that it's an age-related situation. Russia is still unable to accept that, even though Ukraine might be Russia's younger sister, Ukraine has come of old age and is seeking more freedom, independence and more privacy, but above all, respect for the country is smart enough to decide her own destiny and her alliances.

We continue to read in Western media, which is an easily accessible media for us in the world, but there's a clear lack of honesty and exactly as it should be. Western media should be promoting Western propaganda. On the other hand, for Russia it is a matter of making numerous accusations against Ukraine to provide moral support for the invading of a sovereign state is not the best option.

However much Russia loves Ukraine but threat language as well as power that Russia uses is a snare to Ukraine and, yes, Ukraine may be going in a completely wrong direction engaging with Russia, but the truth needs to be expressed with the greatest respect possible in order to stop the stifling of Ukraine will force them even further towards the very hands you want to shield from.

Everybody is today arming Ukraine even though it's intended as Russia protecting their brother. If the proper care isn't taken, Russia could destroy Ukraine or Ukraine could be severely weakened Russia as it reaches its adolescence. combats always end with a manner that was never expected. I can't imagine Russia taking the bitter pill and then resigning, saying they are Russia this is my brother being snooped by I'd like to smack him, I'd like to show him that he's not alone in the wild This is what it's like for Russia.

Russia employed such its iron fists against Ukraine that it appears as if Russia is coming from an perspective of wrath. All I can see is love, excessive love, which pushed Russia to collapse because in destroying Ukraine, Russia is destroying itself. Being from Nigeria me, it might appear that the best way to go is to view things from Western perspectives, since Nigeria is a Western-style democracy and is fond of western values, as the formal British Colony but, since neutrality is due to both sides. I could have tried to imagine Russia in the form of an enclave that is determined to snatch any freedom it can from its citizens and neighbors; however I'm not judging Russia by the rules I have set for it I'm a firm person who believes in the western democratic ideals and principles, but this isn't about the value of western-style democracy. We are talking about a people who chose war over other to protect their ideals.

The impact on the economy of the Western-allied Ukraine is another major issue for Russia and is a major contributor to the list of Russian angry.

It is not due to a communist-style democracy or the consequence of a dictatorial-style management style. Russia's misfortune is, as she is, the only legitimate contestants on the stage of world influence and the competitive inclinations when compared to those of United States of America and its allies.

Even though Russia might seem to be a bit aggressive, it may might be our assumption that we can understand the agressive nature of how powerhouses protect their respective spheres. I'm not blaming on the United States and its allies for the economic problems of Russia despite being aware of their role in the economic calamity of Russia. It simply is how it works: either you take on the opposition or risk losing your standing.

If Russia enjoyed significant economic success and had significant economic success, there could be no way that the United States especially and her allies would be a the world's dominant power for very long. The main factor that keeps America in the top spot is that United States in that position is not only the Military that is, in fact, one of the strongest in the world, but more than all, an enormous economic power.

We can consider Russia as an ally against all chances, attempting to make it through an extremely unfriendly world of economics where the most shots are made by adversaries. Russia isn't in the same league like China or India however the reality lies in the fact that China is a larger market, and besides basic materials Russia isn't able to have the same volume of trade in the same way that China is, in this instance, aside from the raw materials, Russia is economically disposable but I cannot claim the same for China because there's cheap labor available as well as a huge market and the most efficient system of economics. From a business perspective, China is not as easily disposable, particularly on the Asian continent.

The second rival interest to Russia is much more important in terms of economic importance than Russia is, for example, within Europe, European Union is an enormous competitor to Russia while it is the European Union is of more economic significance than Russia in terms of mineral resources. however, this is not the situation in Asia There is no other group or country is a rival to China economically aside from perhaps Japan and Japan isn't currently in the same degree of economic significance with China In this instance we can see that China is the dominant force in Asia economically but that odds in favor of Russia in Europe are just too great We can observe Germany, United Kingdom and France offering Russia an opportunity to run for money, at least in terms of economics involved, there's any way to allow Russia to be a major player. Europe is a very highly competitive continent. If we consider that Russia expands to Asia as well, it is true that within Asia we have China, Japan, South Korea and India each of which could easily strip Russia out of business This is happening in a period when there are constant sanctions on Russia.

Russia is a country with less dominance over its economy. This is partly due to its geographical position. Russia It is not situated in Europe or Asia While the competition within Europe is immense however, the competition in Asia is not any more. It is likely that the United States, China, Japan, Germany, UK etc. will be considered in the event of any attempt to make the world a global. Russia is a country with more secondary economic implications for the continent, which has influenced her projections for international expansion.

If you win China in the game of global economics and she would then crawl back to Asia and if you beat Germany or UK the two would then return to Europe. Outside of raw exports the economic significance is most pronounced throughout Eastern Europe, where there are numerous poverty-stricken nations.

Russia has done fairly well, but there's no any magic in it. Russia is in the midst of aggressive economies from all directions. On the other side are that of the United States. If sanctions were not in place, Russia would have faced the most difficult times with economic advancements.

With all the economic woes and gloom, Russia can't help seeing another country launch a strong resistance in the Eastern

Europe corridors and bring into the west competitors. It's beyond just military implications on Russia and Putin In the long term there will be economic implications for Ukraine when it comes to battling its position in the Eastern European economy. All of these are reasons to the issue.

Whatever way Russia considered it, from any perspective, a independent, democratic, free and independent Ukraine is a risk to Russia and is therefore an ongoing refuge under Russian fears over Ukraine and the war on economics in addition to who will rule Eastern Europe economically, whether it's Russia or Ukraine is a possibility Russia isn't prepared to accept. Ukraine however, isn't willing to let go of her efforts to control Eastern Europe economically and maybe beyond , especially in the event that the odds are favorable for her, even in terms of economics there is no reason to believe that this conflict could not take place.

Chapter 5: Inspirations from China

The body language spoken by China is a fake signal which deceived Russia to believe that China is a foe to China. United States.

In analyzing China's often aggressive rhetoric towards America, United States, we may consider the idea that China is the main adversary for the United States; however, China as well as both the United States are playing a mind game with the rest of the world for the sake of keeping Eastern Asia peaceful, China enjoys an undeserved position that is still able to be removed if she stray, China is a secret admirer of the United States and more than anybody else China loves America. United States as such China would rather remain neutral or have an partnership to China to a practical alliance with the United States however this would never be revealed.

One of the characteristics that is unique to China is that they're not short of memories. China is a mighty country today, however, China will never forget the generosity that is America. United States and while trying to protect her own country, China is a coded country that is pro-America.

China considers itself an economic rival to China and the United States and not an adversary. China has a debt of sovereignty, independence and freedom in the United States. China is aware it is the United States is the primary source of stability within the East Asia corridor; China will most likely not act against American interests; ultimately, American interest is also Chinese interest.

China did not forget World War II, that American protectionism is what secured her sovereignty. Also, China was not forgetting Manchuria and the invasion of Japan. China realizes that she was among the main reasons America was attacked in the Pearl Harbor attack that made America to join World War II. Japan continues to be a major player in the world with the most advanced technologies, both in the military and industry-wise, and is arguably superior to China herself. Japan continues to pose a threat to China All it would require is to Japan to acquire nuclear weapons, and to dismantle the legacy of the World War II agreement, and Eastern Asia is up with another tense situation.

The decision to allow Japan to purchase nuclear warheads and then violate the agreement rests entirely with the United States; that's not something China would like to see. If there is a country that needs peace throughout the world, it's China because if we go to war at some point, China will be the one to suffer the most.

There is absolutely no strategic reason in China to establish a genuine alliance with Russia other than in the event of war. However, China is a cautious nation and, above all else, respects the sovereignty of other nations throughout history, China has had wars with the various dynasties, and building an unifying China was her main ambition, not fighting an extremely powerful foe who do not pose a risk to Chinese people.

China isn't prepared to be caught into an arms war, which is what an association with Russia could imply. Unlike Russia the biggest portion of China's goods exports aren't weapons, therefore China isn't looking to join the arms trade race as utility exports account for the largest part of China's exports. Also, China does not care about global security, she simply would like to be self-sufficient possess enough deterrents, control the economy, and take care of her business. Russia will bring conflict to the table, which China is more averse to than anything else. China too would collapse as it has always been the case and its fragments will be subject to another setback from the robust neighbors.

You might think that the dispute between Taiwan or Hong Kong is enough to cause China enter into an arm-to-arms battle; however I'm not saying China will not be taking this step, however China determines the cost. China knows the circumstances of Taiwan better than any other and the issue with Taiwan isn't America's support or the war talk The issue is that Taiwan would prefer to be left alone.

Through time, China has had some of the sharpest internal generals. They are currently avoiding Taiwan in no way because of the resolve from outside, but due to the internal resolve. Taiwan isn't ready to be integrated fully with the remainder of China as a any forceful integration will eventually have the same consequences that China isn't likely to test, perhaps but not in the near future.

In the instance that of South China Sea, China realizes that she is cheating, therefore in all of these instances, China would prefer to use trade-related rhetoric to show the readiness to launch an attack, but in reality, China is not prepared for any kind of conflict, China knows what she will be fighting against her old enemies if these events get out of hand. China is extremely grateful towards America. United States; they may not express it publicly, however, they do and therefore will not join an alliance of armed inspiration with Russia against the wishes that of United States and its allies.

Russia isn't well-adjusted to China's self-defense style and this makes confrontation the best option for her self-defense determination.

We've witnessed China as a comparable country, with Russia using different strategies to shield herself from various kinds of western influence. for Russia to be a part of the Chinese approach is not feasible as China is located in Asia is an extremely safe place as the majority of Asian countries have similar culturesthat they are proud of. South Korea, Japan and even China might have borrowed the essential elements of western culture; however they have their own influence, and the culture is maintained, they exhibit their culture in a variety of ways like their movies as well as their architecture and various industries that attract worldwide attention. For Russia however, the capability to exert such influence has been removed.

The West does not pay attention to Russia and a large portion of Eastern Europe. Despite the many groundbreaking achievements of Russia but she doesn't seem receive the respect she deserves. The majority of the time, Russia had blamed her loss on an attack by the West and all the other however, Russia might be right and perhaps Eastern Europe civilization could be worthy of more attention. I doubt that an aggressive approach towards Ukraine could have helped her understand Russia's motives.

Russia has a leading position in many aspects of global development however, we hear only about Russia's arsenal in weapon that are used for mass destruction. Russia is a pioneer in space exploration, however we hear more about NASA in the past. Russia is the very first nation to send a person into space. Russia itself could be the one responsible for her negative image, unless the conflict with Russia was long-running and systematic. Usually, Russia herself is to blame since she has a tendency to focus on the display the strength of its military in lieu of all the beauty that she is a symbol of, like hope for the poor nations that are part of Eastern Europe and formal USSR countries. Russia's blazing display of power can be a frightening sight for the less powerful countries and especially the official USSR countries.

Chapter 6: the Fears in This War Rationality Vs. Phobia

Third World War permutation is an unfounded hysteria created by Nuclear anti-Nuclear alarmists.

The incorrect assumption that the war with Ukraine could be a source of source of inspiration for the Third World War which would be Nuclear is more of an alarmist inclination that Putin uses to make everyone shiver. Putin has a strong guy but he is also a respected one, as everyone else, perhaps in the dark hours of the night, in the dark recesses of his thoughts it is possible that he will be possessed by anxiety, and he also is a victim of a price isn't ready to pay, let's say the price is Russia herself.

The truth is that the age that was World War is over; perhaps we can refer to it as the Cosmic War then; the reality is that nuclear conflict can't be a world-wide war, and a war that isn't a world-wide one can't be nuclear. The majority of people worry that Russia and the Ukraine crisis could escalate into a global war but we are unaware that the advent of Nuclear weapons at the end in WW II brought a mechanism that could stop wars in the world but not stopping the war completely.

For a world war to be a reality must be conventional, but nuclear war will be unlike the last time we've seen it It has a cosmic impact not so much due to its human injuries, but rather because of the speed, light and power involved.

If it is to be a war, or a worldwide war, there have to be certain characteristics that are expected, such as troop movement, transport of weapons and a meeting the battleground but in the event of nuclear war, all of these are not necessary. There will be no necessity for a battlefront. each side will sit back in their respective countries and send missiles with nuclear warheads. This eliminates all the characteristics of earlier wars. The war would be remote and weapons will be transported by rockets traveling far beyond what the sound of a single note with massive explosions and light sources we've not seen before, along with extremely fast traveling and penetrating radiation.

A majority of warheads would have to be destroyed by the sea and we will not know the fate of our planet. The only notion we've been told about the nuclear apocalypse has been theorizing and not actual knowledge. Only two explosions of nuclear weapons had been carried out in a war situation, we could witness thousands of explosions within an hour or less but before we could be able to evaluate the situation and declare it the war majority, we could be observing the universe's response against the threat posed by humans, we might consider that nuclear conflict is ours to fight but the planet could be in danger, but it's not a war, it's an invitation or attack to the interests of the universe. The universe might respond or fight back in ways we do not think of as the universe is made of matter and energy when we ask the universe to live and we realize that we're not even more than we believe.

Putin can only be capable of launching a world conflict or nuclear war and not both at the same moment; however it is possible that we begin by expanding the war, and then an nuclear war occur further down the line; but before it escalates to a world war there may not be enough time to decide whether it was a conflict or just a moment of noise from space, World War and Nuclear War cannot happen in tandem, and so Putin has only one choice should he decide to take on the world at any must choose a war with the world or nuclear war, or choose to be self-confident enough to focus on his battle with Ukraine.

If Russia used Nuclear Weapons, we could be witnessing the possibility of a Nuclear Genocide or a different Planet.

The threat from Putin to Nuclear deterrent is absurd; what is the best way to threaten an nuclear scenario while fighting against a non-nuclear power who has surrendered her weapons arsenal of nuclear to Russia and, therefore, Russia isn't threatening Ukraine with a Nuclear Strike, Russia is in danger of with the United States and once there is even a single Nuclear launch against the United States, not only could the US respond, but it would be much easier to the US to stop Nuclear warheads that come via Russia; Russia, on the contrary, would need to fight on the ground and then stop Warheads that came from various parts of the globe would be a frightening scenario. weapons would be arriving through Europe, US, UK and France all at once. Would Russia find it possible to stop these? The size of Russia's area of land means that the majority of the missiles will end up in Russia.

What happens if China as well as North Korea stand by Russia in the event of nuclear conflict? It's very unlikely. North Korea would however, prefer to strike Japan and China would rather maintain peaceful relations within China's East instead of joining forces with Russia or a nation like Israel is likely to be subjected to a swarm of threats from enemies, perhaps India might escalate its war with Pakistan and it could be unorganized, with multiple sides involved and it's going to be insane however, Russia could be facing a real genocidal crisis and for the most part and would remain on her own and NATO will stand in a united front. when there was trouble to China's East, China would find reasons to play the role of peacekeeper rather than involving itself in the larger picture. However it is not a surprise that China and the United States and the NATO allies protect Japan in the context of the Nuclear agreement, should North Korea not behave herself in a way that would get China involved. This is likely to be a bizarre scenario however, once we are certain that this is the case, let up to 24 hours before the war is over. Is enough time to declare war or simply getting up to a brand new world that is clearly damaged, or as likely, a world with completely new forms.

Chapter 7: Russia as a Global Player

Russia kept the modern World Clean

The world is aware the fact that Russia is a powerful nation, a real world power , and an exceptional one. Russia is in a position to stand on its own It is possible to say that Russia is able to continue without the rest of the world, even although the world could proceed without Russia and it could be a very painful experience I do not believe that the world as being capable of advancing without Russia If the world did to do so, and it would have real consequences. The reality is that Russia was able to protect the world more than we believed On the other hand, Russia would find it very difficult to remain in a state of complete isolation.

There are some very ambitious goals in the world that Russia has been shielding the majority of us from. The only power on the planet isn't only NATO and China and China, there's OPEC out there with the intent to dominate and sustain the global crude oil supply Thanks to Russia for all of the time we have been protected from sharks Nigeria as well as China. Russia has a dissuasion that just Russia is able to resist, and the release of oil reserves won't provide any long-term solution and we must come up with a solution to end the war and establish peace with Russia Every country is worried despite economic sanctions imposed on Russia it doesn't seem to be the case that Russia will be suffering more than the nations that have sanctioned, United States needs the oil, Germany needs the gas, Japan needs Russia in quick time and so on. Whatever way we see the situation, we must be peaceful and a solution to the conflict. If Russia continues to fight with Ukraine which is assuming that everyone else is securing Russia and that even Ukraine isn't in a position to conduct business, which would put the world's energy at the hands of OPEC that is comprised of highly smart countries.

Russia is playing itself in Game of Power with So Many Emotions

In a country as strong as Russia being able to play games of power using emotion is laughable. However, emotions are a valid option, but they are not among the strongest. The games of emotion typically favor weaker nations, and not a powerful nation like Russia. Russia is crying when she gets paid in coins, but she believes that just because America did it, everyone can do it. when the USSR utilized Fidel Castro in Cuba, a close-by state of Cuba to afflict America, the United States, everyone cheered USSR however when America chose to utilize Ukraine to afflict Russia and then start to lash out, they begin crying in anger.

In the media, propaganda is circulated about how America attacked the country of that name and the world was looking at other countries, in order in order to defend the involvement of Ukraine. This is because the United States is a country that is a powerhouse and typically infamous for its conduct but power has never been used in a more generous way.

The world didn't ignore the fact that America attacked these nations; the only ones who remained silent and ought to be held accountable are those with the ability to stop America and the ones who should be held accountable the for American brutality are those from countries such as Russia or China.

America always works with other NATO members. If anyone else in the world could be a barrier to NATO interests, who could stand in the way of NATO members and United States and her numerous allies, whenever we promote these kinds of emotional messages Then I ask who are the world's leaders, should there is a time when the United States invades a country regardless of the reason, and China turns away, while Russia turns away the only option of Justice is God as no one has been in a position to hold responsible the United States and her allies accountable and it's the case with the power.

The two countries that are at the top are criminal partners only for a brief moment where there is a real danger of harm being incurred from one powerful country to the next We see a complete refusal since they are the people who fully comprehend their dark scheme; after all, they're the only ones to fully comprehend the utter evil of their powers. That's why they will never allow any other country to be within their borders. If not, then what reason should Russia be concerned about the possibility that America or NATO has Ukraine as a friend within her borders? During the invading of Libya was in progress and what action did Russia do to assist, the delineation of areas of interest is like a race for the entire world, but even when we all have to assume that the situation is fair and we must acknowledge that this expansion is a human condition. Then we consider it to be the totality of power and power play. free of emotions and the notion of victimhood. We look at it at it from the perspective of the statistics and their results.

The reality is that Russia must accept that she's not on the same with that of the United States of America. America is just as formidable than China and Russia when they are together. However, a team made up of China and Russia is able to take on America perhaps in conventional warfare , possibly in a unique style in which all allies and everyone else will stay in and be able to watch a single group consisting of China and Russia fighting America and Russia. The likelihood is that they will win in the United States but not in international politics. America is a formidable advantage.

America is a competitor to Russia in the Military, but is in a battle with China in the economy but, in terms of the international relationship I don't think China or Russia has a chance, perhaps we can look at as well the United Kingdom as a rival to America in international relations and in fact, that the UK is a good partner to America. United States, the fact is that America is pretty completely represented in every sphere of our lives that are important.

Global Economic Scope of the War Global Economic Scope of the War

There is now the start of an Economic World War; each country that sanctions Russia was shot in the leg; it isn't the type that Battle the World Wants.

It is important to acknowledge the reality that Russia is extremely important to the global community to keep the world balanced. Russia keeps the world in balance better than any other nation around the globe. China isn't able to hold the globe in equilibrium, United States can't keep the world in balance with force. Russia is the only one with all tools to keep diplomacy in order, Russia is going to look China in the face, Russia is going to stare at the United States in the eyes, Russia is going to take on the bluff that is NATO, Russia would stand against OPEC, Russia can square the game with the European Union all without really having to fire one shot. The reality is the United States had used more force to achieve their goals than Russia ever has, therefore, we must give Russia an honest assessment and ask why Russia so irritable with Ukraine Why would Russia be so determined to invade Ukraine regardless of all the negotiation capability at her reach.

Aren't we already engaged in a global war or is the entire planet not currently fighting for its own survival by fighting Russia in the form of countries placing self-harming sanctions on Russia and yet there's no other alternative to Russia. The world cannot wait to greet Russia back. There are only a handful of countries which can live without Russia When we look at nations like China and India, a few of their deals are tied with those of the United States the impact of increasing oil prices for those in the United States and the consequential economic impacts would have implications to many countries. China too would be affected, and nearly all of the world could be affected.

Perhaps African countries might be less affected because Africa as an area is enjoying some independence as well as less integration the world, but most African countries, just like Nigeria are incredibly unreliable.

Russia Will Not Stay the same, and neither would anyone else, in particular Ukraine.

The only thing that I can tell is that is different in Russia in that it is there appear to be a lot of sanctions for Russia and there is a lot of destruction and suffering in Ukraine and the majority of the world particularly NATO nations as well as European Union Countries, there are also consequences.

Sometimes, we consider the sanctions imposed on Russia and we think Russia and Russia only would be affected and we ignore the fact that Russia is a full part of the global community , and an extremely powerful one at this.

If NATO or American allies insist on sanctioning Russia in the name of sanctions, then we tend to ignore the fact that the relation with Russia with the other countries hadn't been one of total dependence and it is likely that there was not even a form of dependence, Russia had been engaging solely on the basis of business and mutually beneficial relationships to the other nations.

It's not like the world has agreements with Russia without cost. It's always been business with Russia and when you recognize Russia in a system where Russia is a leading performer in a few key sectors that we're disrupting the international system, we change the course of global functioning and will most likely result in consequences for the vast majority.

Ukraine itself might be able to keep the world going even if Russia needed to be eliminated, but Ukraine is in the middle of the chaos. Therefore, currently there isn't anyone as Russia each country is different, but certain countries have more.

Russia in a broad sense is unalterable at present. It is possible to see the USA as being cut off from the world. But for the most part. China, UK, Germany and Canada are able to provide the world with everything we might be lacking within America. United States; if China is not in the picture and the world is in a state of chaos, Japan, South Korea and the United States can confidently push the world ahead, however should we were to cut Russia off, perhaps with the assistance by Ukraine there is a chance to achieve remained in the balance, particularly in Europe and the Middle East. However, both Ukraine as well as Russia will be isolated and the world is not ready for Russia or countries that resemble Russia The only alternative alternative to Russia is Russia threat and the world wouldn't be able to have Ukraine without Russia The earlier we realize the delicate nature of the situation of Russia the more we will understand the situation.

The Motives and Calculations of Putin the man of the War

Putin is fighting the psychological war, and not just playing with the psychological issues of Ukraine but also creating the psychological environment of Russians as well as the world community.

There are various phases to Putin's theories that seem almost impossible to not be a part of his scripts. He has came up with so many ideas that they're all unfolding simultaneously, regardless of how you see it. Putin is the one who calls the shots in this conflict.

He has his own opinions and almost everyone behaves in line with his ideas, however this does not necessarily mean that he has complete control. It implies that in one manner or another there would be a an end-to-end justification. However how the situation is taking place, there would remain a definitive justification, though perhaps not as you would like or expected. Putin himself could have somewhat unexpected outcomes.

The first calculation: Putin prepared for every scenario, with the reverse results. He prepared for a shorter campaign, as well as a longer campaign in preparation for small casualties, and prepared for the possibility of wanton casualties. prepared for speed, ready for delay, prepared the toughest of opposition and also planned for a win easily, which is surprising considering Putin is ready for defeat, but Putin isn't prepared to concede defeat completely.

Second calculation: Putin is prepared to demonstrate to Russians the risk of not allowing Ukraine an unfettered hand and especially a long-term relationship with NATO. This is expected to happen as a outcome of a massive either directly or indirectly by NATO as well as other NATO allies. This would be accompanied by a price that could result in a massive opposition and a potential loss to Russia and this could justify the invasion, as the most people in Russia will be able to be able to clearly perceive how big of an issue a western and NATO allies Ukraine could pose, while showing this would have an expensive price.

In this case, prior, Putin commanded the most significant military operation ever since World War II, at the staggering rate of building and the only method Ukraine was to withstand that massive military incursion is to do so with the aid of something even more powerful and in this instance, NATO whether directly or indirectly.

Putin wants to prove that an independent, western-allied independently Ukraine is as harmful to Russia like any other enemy. It is clear that Ukraine could not have stood up to this level of attack on her own. Even accurate and timely intelligence is vital and crucial in all these instances, Ukraine is seemingly incapable of standing up to Russia however, what is it that she's doing so effectively? There isn't any other explanation for the second calculation, Putin is getting the desired results here. An integrated Ukraine is a risk for Russia.

The opposite: Ukraine stands entirely alone and the result is a simple win for Russia. Putin has yet to get the desired outcome. NATO and their allies provoked Ukraine to war , and then left her. If that was not the situation, Putin could have either employed a more humane strategy to bring Ukraine closer to one another, as Belarus leader advised Zelensky to make an apology Putin and could have happened however, there is the possibility of balancing events, and, even in the present, and the war is still raging.

Calculation 3: Putin is prepared for the worst and is ready for a minimally damaged world. More resistance means further damage but the war isn't likely to be over until something catastrophic happens, and is currently unknown. knows what that might be. The reality is that Russia isn't fighting at all, but is creating destruction in Ukraine and until Putin realizes the consequences go that goes beyond sanctions, there's no resolution to this issue.

Russia is profiting from this Covid 19 New Beginning.

It might have made sense in the event that Russia had been fighting wars or being subject to sanctions however, Russia is going on an extremely cheap war and the world as well as Russia is suffering. It is possible to think that fighting war and maintaining an economically viable and functioning economy could not be easy but, Russia is not fighting any war. So, what are Russia fighting when there is no Russian city is affected or impacted, and there is no Russian interest is harmed, aside from sanctions Russia does not feel any kind of hit, it's just troops dying and weapons which had been put in the defence budget.

This war's cost is inexpensive for Russia and this war comes just as there could be a chance of the possibility of a new beginning for everyone based on the effects on the world of Covid 19 in the globe; the world was not moving forward and had not accounted for the true damages of Covid 19; we had hoped for a new, unified world. Russia would like to begin with the beginning of a new chapter.

Covid 19 had believed in everyone's self-sufficiency was a virtue and made a sham situation for a lot of people; Russia has learned to deal with restrictions or the world that decided to remain silent. Russia is now standing still in the world and we hope that when Russia is done with her provocations everything or a few things will return to how it was.

The same thing happens as during the Covid 19 lockdown; everyone is inside, but everyone is eager to go out. The severe sanctions on Russia affects the countries who have sanctioned Russia more than Russia however, when we consider the general pain from these sanctions into account, Russia is suffering more than all countries , but each of the countries which approved Russia is suffering the loss from Russia in a way that is greater than Russia herself.

Russia is not too worried as covid 19 has brought the world into a new era, it is the responsibility of Russia to start afresh instead of trying to maintain the old one, which is not the same.

The fate of Ukraine

What happens to Ukraine is in the balance but it's an incredibly painful and destruction. The length of time they will last remains to be determined, but one thing is certain nobody has predicted the future in any way. It might appear like the case that if they linger for longer and the patterns may alter however Putin has the world to himself. to be, so long as everything continues to move as it is in the near future, the future is impossible to predict for Ukraine.

Does it appear as if Russia is in the middle of an War?

To Russia it seems that what is going on in Ukraine isn't a war as Putin believes that it is a unique package designed for achieving specific goals. the reality is that there is conflict inside Ukraine and sanctions from time to time but regardless of the extent to which the West supports Ukraine; Ukraine is suffering.

Russia might have a large percentage of their combat forces, but, not all soldiers would be able to survive to the ravages of war; many would come back alive following the battle. which is why the weapon is a thing that Russia have on hand and we should be aware that in the case of suffering, Russia is not alone.

In truth, NATO may not have moral obligations towards Ukraine.

The reality is NATO has acted on ill will of Russia and not based on affection for Ukraine, NATO is not planning to save Ukraine but is thinking about taking on Russia in the event that Ukraine returns to her senses in this war, she's not even part of a conflict that had been so devastating for Ukraine In reality the world, there's not much concern for Ukraine and that's the reason this war could be very dangerous for her. NATO perceives Russia and Russia perceives NATO which then turns its attention to Ukraine.

With Russia each sanction is a counter-sanction and, therefore, Ukraine should not rely on Sanctions.

When you sanctioned Russia it, you self-sanctioned because the countries that sanction Russia as well as Russia were both beneficiaries of the earlier status quo; however, the sanctions against Russia could be detrimental to Ukraine further since this could cause global turmoil and Ukraine will be unable to deal with the global turmoil as it fights a devastating conflict.

The Verdict on Russia and Ukraine. Verdict about Russia and Ukraine

No matter how you look into it Russia can be brutal, and aggressive with a long-term strategy to destroy Ukraine and Ukraine however is a sly infiltrator that has a long-term Strategy to Defend Russia

We can't have a complete picture if we do not look at the past of Russia and Ukraine in the years since the establishment of the sovereignty of Ukraine has been questioned, but there's a veiled plan of Russia to eliminate and take over Ukraine and on the other hand, from the perspective of Ukraine there is an unorthodox strategy to subvert Russia in order to undermine Russia Russian interests. There has also been a deliberate incursion into Ukraine as both countries claim to see the other as a sister state.

It might appear that an ideally harmonious relationship could be likely for Russia and Ukraine but in the real world, Russia is ready to sacrifice everything in the name of global power and politics. however, Ukraine is not prepared to let go of her sinister motives in opposition to Russia and Ukraine. There must be the opportunity to compromise as soon as is possible. Otherwise should these two countries keep unleashing the devil they are preparing against each other it could lead to an utterly inhumane situation on a world-wide magnitude.

Chapter 8: The Reasons is There a War?

The Russo-Ukrainian War is a long-running conflict that involves Russia and pro-Russian forces and Belarus on one side in addition to Ukraine and Ukraine on the other. The conflict between the two countries in Ukraine started in February 2014 when the majority of the country's southern and eastern areas (the Donetsk, Lugansk, and Crimea) were occupied by forces from Russia. Russian Federation. The war is referred to by the name of War in Donbas (2014-present) known for its sometimes-unlawful nature of the conflict that has also involved the involvement from foreign forces. There have been numerous allegations of incidents that have impacted other countries, including the tank attack in Estonia in April of 2016. Unrest within the Iriao region also arises from the conflict. In the years prior to when these events happened but, there has been tensions in the region between Russia and Ukraine regarding gas prices and political ideologies. Russia has provided military support to rebels in Donbas as it tried to conceal its involvement. In the last quarter of 2021, a significant army has been established at the border. The 24th of February, 2022 the president Putin began a massive assault on Ukraine. In the aftermath of events like the Euromaidan incidents, Ukrainian President Viktor Yanukovych was forced to step down in 2014. A portion of Ukraine saw an increase in the pro-Russian tensions. Russian soldiers with no emblems took over strategically important positions and infrastructure within Ukraine's Crimea. The Russian Federation Council voted unanimously on March 1 to request Russian the President Vladimir Putin to use military force in Ukraine. Unknown Russian forces stormed the Crimean Parliament and Russia held a widely-criticized referendum, the outcome of which was Crimea's entry into Russia. Pro-Russian protests across Ukraine's Donbas region began in April, resulting in an uneasy war in the region between Ukrainian military and Russian-backed separatists of the self-proclaimed Donetsk as well as Luhansk republics. The unmarked Russian army vehicles crossed to Donetsk republic in August. Donetsk republic during August. this was blamed as the reason on Ukrainian force being defeated by the beginning of September. It was reported that the Special Monitoring Mission of the Organization for Security and Cooperation in Europe (OSCE) has reported convoys of unmarked soldiers and heavy weapons in the separatist-held Donbas during November of 2014 that were claimed by the Ukrainian military claimed originated from Russia. OSCE monitors have also reported seeing vehicles carrying ammunition disguised as aid convoys for humanitarian purposes, as well as soldiers who had been killed during combat being brought back to Russia. In a story from Moscow Times, It is not a secret that Russia has repressed and intimidated human rights activists who reported the deaths and losses of Russian soldiers fighting in the conflict.

Who is Vladimir Putin?

Putin is the Russian president of Russia. Putin was born the 7th of October 1952 at Leningrad (now Saint Petersburg), Russia. He was raised in a shared apartment with his parents, going to local high and grammar schools, and gaining an fascination with sports. Putin was recruited by in the KGB in the capacity of an intelligence agent following his graduation of Leningrad State University with a law degree in the year. He was in that post predominantly located in East Germany, until 1990 at which point he was discharged as a lieutenant colonel. Putin was then back in Russia and became administrative director for Leningrad's University of Leningrad before becoming an advisor for Liberal politician Anatoly Sobchak after communism fell in 1991. Putin was appointed Sobchak's chief of foreign relations after the mayor was elected to Leningrad later in the year and in 1994, he was been named Sobchak's deputy mayor for the first time. Putin left his post and moved to Moscow following the defeat of Sobchak in 1996. Putin was named the deputy chief of staff for Boris Yeltsin's administration in 1998. Putin was in charge of the Kremlin's relationships with regional authorities in that capacity. Boris Yeltsin, who was the Russian president at the time, fired his premier Sergei Stepashin and replaced him with an ex KGB agent Vladimir Putin. Yeltsin quit in December 1999 and appointed Putin as president. He was elected again in 2004. Putin made a historic trip in Israel during April of 2005. It was marking the first visit by any Kremlin leader. Putin could not contest the presidency again in 2008, however Putin was appointed the prime minister by his successor Dmitry Medvedev. Putin was elected at the end of March in 2012 to be president and then re-elected the fourth time.

Who exactly is Volodymyr Zelensky?

It is Ukrainian president of Ukraine. On the 25th of January 1978 his birthplace was in Jewish parents from Kryvyi Rih, Ukraine, that was then an integral part of the Soviet Union, to Rimma Zelenskaya who was an engineer and Oleksandr Zelensky who was a professor and director of the Department of Cybernetics and Computing Hardware at the Kryvyi Rih Institute of Economics. He was a lawyer but chose to go into comedy which was a huge success. His political humor has been compared with Jon Stewart's. He was the winner of the Ukrainian comedy contest, and then went on to create and appear in a variety of television and film productions through Kvartal 95, his production company. Kvartal 95. He has been a vocal opponent of the bans imposed by Ukraine on Russian performers, and, as a result one of his film, Love In the Big City 2 was shut down in his country. After Zelensky and his company contributed funds towards the Ukrainian army in the past, certain Russian authorities requested that his work be restricted in Russia also. in 2015 Zelensky was a part of the TV show Servant of the People as teacher who was elected as the president of Ukraine following a viral video in which he denounces government corruption went viral via social media.

What are the motives of Russia for the war?

In a pre-dawn, telecast address, Russian President Vladimir Putin declared that Russia did not be confident that it is "safe to develop, grow, or exist" due to the constant threat from the modern Ukraine. Military headquarters and airports were immediately attacked, and then by troops and tanks from Russia and which annexed Crimea with the help of its Allies Belarus. Major cities have been targeted and destroyed, as well as neighborhoods thousands of Ukrainians have evacuated their home. Yet, Russia outlaws the terms "war" and "invasion," and threatens journalists with imprisonment when they employ the terms. This is an "special action by the military" according to the president Vladimir Putin. Many of his war excuses were either illogical or false. The reason he claimed to be in war was to protect people who were bullied or victims of genocide as well as "demilitarize and remove the Nazification of" Ukraine. There has never been a genocide or massacre in Ukraine which is a flourishing democratic state ruled by the president of Ukraine, a Jewish president.

"How do I become the definition of a Nazi?" was the question asked by Volodymyr Zelensky. He described Russia's military invasion as Nazi Germany's invasion of the Second World War. The slander of Russia was also rebuffed by Ukraine's head Rabbi and The Auschwitz Memorial. Since Ukraine's pro-Russian President, Viktor Yanukovych, was removed in 2014 following several months of demonstrations in protest against his administration and the president Putin frequently said that Ukraine is being controlled by extremists. Ukraine however, on the other side, has been unwilling to change its kremlin position and instead has been a shift towards the west and vladimir Putin would like to alter the way it views. When Russia pressured Ukraine's President to not sign an agreement to join the European Union, protests erupted. This year, Russia took Crimea's southern region and triggering an uprising in the east, assisting rebels fighting Ukrainian forces in a war that lasted for eight years and has claimed more than 14,000 lives. Ukraine has expressed an interest in becoming a member of the EU as well as NATO however the powerhouses within the Kremlin are not letting it occur. Russia began to build huge numbers of troops near the borders of Ukraine in the latter part of 2021. President Putin has denied plans to invade, but he later renounced his 2015 Minsk peace accord for the eastern region and acknowledged the territories controlled by rebels as independent. He also accused NATO of threatening "our long-standing future as an entire nation" by bringing in the military.

What is Putin really want? And how much will he go?

The president Vladimir Putin has made it evident that he would like to take over Ukraine and overthrow the government that is democratically elected. "The enemy has designated me as the number one target and my family as second in line," President Zelensky added. The declared objective of Russia is to see Ukraine to be freed from oppression as well as "cleansed from Nazis." President Putin has promised to bring the guilty to trial "those who have committed a variety of horrendous crimes against the people" within this false narrative of a fascist-ruled Ukraine since 2014. He has repeatedly denied any attempt to take over Ukraine and has denied an UK claim that he planned to set up a Kremlin puppet prior to the war, however, he also has said that there will not be an invasion. In a report on intelligence issued by the pentagon, Putin is planning to split Ukraine in half. Even though Russia's Baltic neighbors are not currently under threats, Nato has reinforced their defenses to be ready in the event of. The writer has praised a brand new global order that Russia was rebuilding the prior Soviet unity, and bringing together what is known as the Russian community comprised of Russians, Belarusians, and Little Russians, in an editorial that was published on February 26 and later deleted by the state-owned news agency Ria-Novosti in which the author praised a new global order that Russia restored the prior Soviet unity, and bringing together the"real" Russian world comprised of Russians, Belarusians, and Little Russians (Ukrainians). The president Putin has written a long blog last year that portrayed Russians as well as Ukrainians as "one group," and he has spoken of the collapse of the Soviet Union on December 21, 1991, being the "disintegration of the old Russia."

Vladimir Putin wants Ukraine to recognize Crimea as a part of Russia and also the eastern region run by separatists as independent to put an end to the war. He is also seeking to amend Ukraine's constitution so that it can not be a member of NATO as well as the EU. He also is calling for NATO to return in 1997 to stop the expansion to the east in the belief the claim that Russia has "nowhere else to go" and "do they believe that we'll be passive?" This would mean Nato taking its forces and military installations from the member states that joined the alliance following 1997, and also refusing to deploy "strike weapons" close to Russia's borders. This would include Central as well as Eastern Europe and the Baltic countries. Olaf Scholz, German's chancellor believes that this goes far beyond Nato and says the fact that Vladimir Putin "wants to take control of Europe according to his view of the world." Putin is threatening to establish the foundations of a Russian empire. The West was able to agree in the year 1990 that Nato would extend "not one inch in the direction of the eastern hemisphere," but did so nonetheless, as per the president Putin. But, since this was prior to the Soviet Union's collapse the commitment given to Soviet the president Mikhail Gorbachev only applied to East Germany as part of the reunified Germany. "The issue of NATO expansion was not even considered" in the moment, Gorbachev later said.

How will this conflict affect Europe

Ukrainians live in terror as bombs and shells fall on their cities which has forced more than two million to leave for neighboring countries. Poland, Hungary, Romania, Moldova, and Slovakia are struggling with a massive flow of refugees, and an EU declaring that at the very least five million people are likely to be forced out. This is an important moment with the potential to disrupt Europe's post-World-War II security system. A few days after warning Europe and the West with "consequences similar to those you've never witnessed" should it get within his reach, Russian President Putin has placed his nuclear forces on the alert. This war has reminded Europe of of the most gloomy moments after the conclusion of

World War II. It was the time that French leader, Emmanuel Macron, spoke of a pivotal moment that was a turning point in European history. This is a difficult time for families of both the soldiers and their families. Ukrainians have endured an eight-year war with Russian proxy groups. Reservists from all age groups between the between the ages of 18 to 60 have been drafted from the military. This is not a war to which the Russian citizens were ready, since the war was endorsed by a majority of the unrepresentative lower chamber of the Russian parliament. In a country where the principal opponent was poisoned by an atomic weapon prior to being imprisoned, tens thousands of protesters against war were incarcerated as well as the independent Russian media outlets have had their licenses taken from the broadcasting air.

The 1994 Nuclear Deal assuring Ukrainian sovereignty

Kiev was forced to give the nuclear arsenal in exchange for an Russian promise to defend Ukrainian sovereignty, as per the anti-western Budapest Memorandum. Russia's complete invasion of Ukraine reminds us of the crucial post-Cold war agreement on the nuclear capabilities of Ukraine that was a signatory to Kiev give up its arsenal of nuclear weapons in exchange for promises from both the US and the UK that Moscow will respect the former Soviet sovereignity of the republic.

Ukraine was home to the third largest nuclear arsenal on the planet with at the very least 1,900 nuclear weapons that were strategic. The former communist Soviet republic had left Ukraine with the infrastructure. Its ability could be "more than 6 times more than the amount of nuclear weapons China currently has," according to Steven Pifer who is a non-resident expert at the Brooking Institution and former US ambassador to Ukraine. In the current conflict the strategic capabilities could have had a huge impact, possibly deterring Vladimir Putin from invading

Ukraine and even putting Russian nukes to "high on alert."

Following when the Soviet Union fell apart in 1991 and the United States and the United Kingdom were able to convince Ukraine to surrender its nuclear arsenal to be exchanged for Russia's promise to "maintain Ukraine's sovereignty, independence as well as its boundaries" in the 1994 Budapest Memorandum. Moscow also was able to "refrain from threatening or employing violence" against Ukraine in accordance with the agreement. Russia however, contrary to this is in flagrant violation of the nuclear pact signed in 1994 by its continued assault on Ukraine. "Russia violates its own Budapest Memorandum of 1994, which pledged to protect the sovereignty of Ukraine and its territorial integrity as long as Ukraine had to give up its nuclear arsenal," argues Matthew Bryza an ex- US Ambassador to Azerbaijan, the ex Soviet Azerbaijan republic. Azerbaijan. Moscow has taken part of the Crimean Peninsula, a Black Sea peninsula in the Black

Sea, out of Ukraine at the end of 2014 a long time ahead of the current Russian attack. The same year, pro-Russian separatists seized parts within that region of the Donbass region in the eastern part of Ukraine. Putin recognized the separatist regions in the form of autonomous republics prior the ongoing Russian incursion. Both actions of Russia are flagrantly in violation of Ukrainian sovereignty. "Russia has essentially violated every promise it made in the agreement," Pifer said of the 1994 Memorandum.

Was the West fully committed to this agreement?

Although Russia's annexation Ukrainian territory, the support of rebels, and the most recent invasion could violate the 1994 Memorandum however both the United Kingdom nor the United States have committed to protecting Ukraine by means of arms. This could be a violation of the aggrement of 1994 as well. In Article 5, NATO creates a duty of military to two countries, the US with the UK however this is not the situation in the current situation since Ukraine is not an official member in the alliance transatlantic. However, both the United States and the United Kingdom have fulfilled their obligations to defend Ukraine's sovereignty as well as territorial integrity by providing economic and diplomatic backing and, in particular, with unprecedentedly tough restrictions against Russia. As security assurances were being discussed at Budapest during 1994 US officials said should Russia had violated the agreements they would be retaliated against by the US would be taking a huge risk and would retaliate. In order to distinguish between promises and assurances, they said and guarantees, they claimed that the former needed the American militarily committed. It's not clear what Ukrainians were interpreting US assurances in 1994 or if they were aware of the distinction between guarantees and assurances. "Ukraine was misled in Budapest," according to certain significant American media outlets. Associate professor in the Institute for Russian and Eurasian Studies at Uppsala University, Gregory Simon believes that the Budapest

Memorandum was breached not just by Moscow as well as The United States by using Ukraine as a geopolitical target for its own games. Simon pointed out that the document is a way of highlighting the consequences of a change in the world order, and also of the ways the parties to the conflict are deliberately avoiding formal international agreement and the terms of the treaty.

Treaties; MINSK Agreement

The month of September was when Ukraine as well as separatists backed by Russia agreed to a 12-point ceasefire agreement in the Belarusian capital Minsk. It stipulated prisoner swaps and humanitarian aid deliveries and the abolition of heavy weapons, just five months into a war which had claimed the lives of over 2600 people. That's a number that Ukrainian Presidency Volodymyr Zelenskiy says has been increased to around 15,000 victims. The agreement was immediately dissolved and both sides broke the deal.

MINSK Agreement II

A 13-point agreement was signed in February 2015 by the representatives from Russia, Ukraine, the Organization for Security and Cooperation in Europe (OSCE), and the heads of two separatist districts pro-Russian. In February, the Franch President, Germany chancellor and the Russian as well as Ukraines president and Ukrainian president, all of whom were present at Minsk issued an endorsement of the agreement. The agreement entailed both political and military actions that are not yet implemented. Russia has denied involvement in the conflict , and does not adhere to its terms. This has been an obstacle. For instance, point 10 requires the removal of all foreign military units as well as military gear from both disputable territory that are Donetsk as well as Luhansk; Ukraine claims this is a reference to Russian forces, whereas Moscow has denied having any involvement in the conflict.

The 13 points that were selected included:

1. A quick and complete cease-fire 2.Withdrawal of any heavy weapon, by both sides 3. Dialog on an interim government for Donetsk as well as Luhansk region, in accordance with Ukraines laws and recognize their unique status in a Parliamentary Resolution 4.Monitoring as well as evaluations by OSCE 5. Amnesty and pardoning for those who participated in the conflict 6. exchange of prisoners. Assistance for humanitarian needs 8. Establishment of socioeconomic ties including pensions 9. The restoration of complete control over the border between the states with the help of the Government of Ukraine 10. Elimination of all foreign armies as well as military gear and mercenaries. 11. Amendments to the Constitution in Ukraine which includes decentralization and explicit recognition by Donetsk as well as Luhansk 12. Elections are scheduled in Donetsk and Luhansk with conditions to be negotiated by the respective representatives of 13. As an Trilateral Contact Group made up of representatives from Ukraine Russia, Ukraine along with the OSCE.

What is the reason why the 2015 deal been unable to end the war?

It is believed that the Minsk II agreement stated military and political steps that have yet to be put into effect. Russia is not a party to the conflict , and thus isn't bound by the terms of the agreement, which has proved to be an obstacle. In general the two sides Moscow as well as Kyiv interpret the agreement in a different way which has led to what a an analyst from the west called "Minsk puzzle,".

What is the 'Minsk Conundrum What is the 'Minsk conundrum'?

Ukraine sees the 2015 agreement as a means to regain control of the territory held by rebels. In this context the country seeks a ceasefire and controlling the borders between Russia and Ukraine and election in Donbas and a limited decentralization of power to rebels as well as representation in central administration, which allows Moscow to block Kyiv's foreign policy choices. Then, Russia surrender control over the border between Ukraine and Russia to Kyiv.

The differences in Minsk I and Minsk II

The month of September was the year that Ukraine, Russia, the Organization for Security and Cooperation in Europe (OSCE), Russia, Ukraine and pro-Russia separatists signed the first Minsk agreement. Ukraine and separatists signed to a ceasefire agreement of 12 points that also included the withdrawal of heavy weaponry as well as swapping prisoners. However, despite numerous violations from each side, the deal was not able to resolve the war. Minsk II was signed five months later, following Ukraine lost its territory to separatists from Russia. In February 2015, officials both from Russia and Ukraine came to a 13-point agreement that was negotiated with France along with Germany. The OSCE recorded about 200 weekly violations between 2016 until 2020, and more than 1,000 in 2021 under the second agreement.

What is the reason for the MINSK agreement now in the spotlight could it be a way to end the dispute?

It is believed that the Minsk II agreement provides an opportunity for direct talks that will be held between Ukraine and Russia as well as an opportunity for French president Emmanuel Macron to play peacemaker in the international arena in the run-up to an election in his home country. Russia could see Minsk II as a tool to ensure that Ukraine will not be admitted into NATO as one of Russia's most important security concerns that from the beginning was resisted in the past by Washington as well as NATO.

The MINSK accord may provide an chance for Ukraine to gain control over the border it shares with Russia and reduce the risk of another attack by russia in the least, for the moment. Kyiv has declared that Russia could never exercise the right to veto its foreign policy in Ukraine. Many Ukrainians see Minsk II's enactment as a retaliation against Russian aggression. There could be possibility of compromise since both sides have shown an interest in discussing.

Nuke Threats From Putin

The recent activation of Russian nuclear weapons by President Vladimir Putin has recently heightened tensions in Ukraine and has brought back defence experts like Professor Simons about the events of 1962 Cuban Missile Crisis, when the Soviets placed nuclear warhead missiles in Cuba, a Central American country, posing danger towards US National security. Both sides have learned a lot from the conflict of 1962. "I think both sides are playing a highly risky game of escalation that is followed by counter-escalation, and little discussion. In the months since November, the atmosphere is extremely heated, without anyone pondering the implications for the future," Professor Simons adds in a note that Putin's reasoning might differ from the one of Westerners. "Now Putin has been pushed into a situation in which he has virtually no stake. In his personal life as well as professionally speaking, it means that the calculation of benefits and costs that are a part of US sanctions are no longer valid in a rational way. This makes people extremely unstable." He said.

It's worth noting that Ukraine has given the use of nuclear weapons as a condition of Western security assurances against Russia and is currently in the middle of possible scenarios of nuclear war. Ukraine had nuclear weapons intercontinental ballistic weapons (ICBMs) and strategic bombers prior the Budapest Memorandum of 1994. "The warheads on top of the SS-19 as well as SS-24 ICBMs within Ukraine were explosively yielded at 400-550 kilograms, which is about 35 times the weight of the atomic bomb that destroyed Hiroshima," Pifer wrote in his essay, alluded in reference to United States strike on the Japanese city during the war.

What is the position of NATO?

The North Atlantic Treaty Organization (NATO) has expressed its anger over Russia's incursion into Ukraine by sending the tens of thousands into Eastern Europe to safeguard its members. Although Russian troops have launched an attack that is deadly against Ukraine, NATO member states are not going to take on Russia in a war until any of their member states gets attacked by Russia. The decision to stay clear of conflict comes at an extremely difficult moment for NATO since Ukraine has expressed an desire to join the defence alliance, but was refused entry because of Russia's strong resistance to any the further NATO Eastward expansion. At present, Russia's broad-based offensive against Ukraine is limited to the borders of Ukraine, including bombings and airstrikes targeting military and civilian facilities and cities however, the majority of NATO members are on alert and have asked for the other members to look into whether it is appropriate for the alliance to take collective actions. Russia's actions have been branded "a horrific act of warfare" by NATO Secretary-General Jens Stoltenberg, who also said that the alliance would protect "every millimeter" of its territory if Russia struck any of their members, something experts in the field think is unlikely. Despite the constant combat and increasing loss, NATO is not sending troops to Ukraine instead, opting to build their own east flank.

At a press event the 24th of February, 2022 Stoltenberg declared, "We have no plans to send NATO troops in Ukraine." "We have increased the scope of our efforts to increase their presence NATO soldiers on

NATO territories in the eastern region in the NATO alliance." United States President Joe Biden has confirmed that he will not send troops to Ukraine within hours of when NATO announced its plans. In fact, the US currently has 90,000. troops based in Europe with the majority of them are in Germany and has pledged additional seven hundred troops to the country.

"We can be involved in the event that Russian president Vladimir Putin moves into NATO countries," Biden warned Thursday afternoon. "The positive side is NATO will be stronger and stronger than it's before." But in the midst of Russian troops advanced in their assault on Ukraine overnight, NATO stated that it will send parts of its combat-ready forces in Eastern Europe as a precautionary move at the beginning of its its history. NATO has promised to keep sending weapons to Ukraine and aerial defenses, yet it has not yet committed to sending troops.

NATO and Ukraine

From the arming of Ukrainian soldiers, to providing assistance to the needy, and even imposing sanctions against Russia and its president Vladimir Putin, NATO member nations have taken measures to impede Moscow's progress or provide Kyiv assistance. But, the options of the alliance are limited. Despite accusations of war violations and human rights violations within Ukraine, NATO countries have declared that they will not to directly participate in the conflict , or, in some cases, even being drawn into it, through airspace patrols in Ukraine or placing troops on Ukrainian land, for example. This is because of an amendment to the charter of the military alliance that binds 28 European nations and two North American countries committed to keeping peace and security in the North Atlantic region known as Article. Every attack that targets any of the members in accordance with Article 5, constitutes an attack on all. In the Cold War, when the alliance sought to limit the growth of the Soviet Union, it served as a deterrent. In the present situation, its violation could trigger an escalation that is similar to a nightmare. NATO Secretary General Jens Stoltenberg has stated that NATO partners should "prevent the war from spreading to Ukraine."

Ukraine as well as Georgia was invited be a part of NATO in 2008, provided they satisfied a set of conditions, including NATO's rules of governance and transparency. The Ukrainian desire to be a part of NATO has been a high goal, but the application process has not made much progress. Certain NATO partners blame this delays on the country's past of corruption and others say the transition to democracy in Ukraine that began in the mid-1990s, remains in a state of instability. Some NATO nations are concerned about the possibility that, should Ukraine is accepted into the alliance, Russia would retaliate strongly. According to Ukraine's ambassador in the United Kingdom, Russia has threatened and blackmailed Ukraine over its determination to be a part of NATO. But, Ukraine updated its constitution in the year 2019 to include the aim of full NATO membership, which means that the efforts are likely to be ongoing. Even though NATO has yet to accept Ukraine however, it has helped the country defend itself from Russian aggression. When Russia attacked the eastern part of Ukraine and took over Crimea during 2014 NATO intervened by stopping cooperating with Kyiv and increasing its defensive capabilities. It conducted drills for military, deployed troops into regions, and also provided the funds for cyberwarfare defenses. But, it did not engage militarily in the war.

"We are told that the door is opened," Ukraine President Volodymyr Zelensky declared last week regarding the possibility to join NATO. "But currently it is not possible for outsiders to get to enter."

What are the articles 4 and 5 cover?

Even though experts believe that an attack against NATO members is unlikely at the moment, a few NATO members have asked for security conferences pursuant to article 4 of the NATO Treaty. Article 4 states that "if it is believed that, from the perspective of any one of them, the sovereignty, territorial integrity or security of one of the Parties is at risk," countries "will discuss jointly."

Article 4 consultations do not assure that the action will take place however it allows for rapid discussions. Since the alliance's inception at the time of its founding in 1949 Turkey was a member six times. most recent time in February 2020 after a number of Turkish military personnel suffered fatal injuries at the hands of Syrian military forces within the opposition-held areas northern Syria. At the time, the member countries were not able to make use of Article 5, which states that an attack on a member is as an attack on all other countries in the alliance. In the event that Article 5 is invoked, all NATO countries are required to join forces, most likely to fight if one their members is targeted. The clause has been invoked only one time, following the terrorist attacks that occurred on September 11th 2001. Although NATO has hinted previously that it will defend its members should they be attacked by terrorists, triggering Article 5 would be a significant step towards the development of a clear strategy of actions.

"We will take whatever steps are necessary to protect our alliance from threats,"

Stoltenberg said. "Our collective defense obligation under Article 5 is ironclad."

Does it make sense for an Cyberattack to invoke Article 5?

Since the Russian invasion of Ukraine alertness for cybercrime worldwide has increased and has prompted US officials to warn American businesses and institutions to be prepared for cyberattacks in response to the imposing of tough sanctions against Russia. Analysts are shocked at the lack of major cyberattacks that shut down communication, disrupted power supply, or otherwise hurt the economy of Ukraine even though Russia being able to launch these attacks for years. Some have suggested the Russian attackers were taken out by the attack, or were otherwise not prepared. However, these attacks could happen at any time. When the war began, Stoltenberg indicated that a cyberattack could also cause Article 5, echoing NATO's earlier declaration that the alliance would "fight against any attack on members, virtual or physical." But there's a the possibility that a string of cyberattacks could trigger an unbalanced response, an increase in the earlier. According Sloan, according to Sloan the cyberattacks are an "gray zone" according to Article 5, depending on the seriousness or severity of an attack, and whether it is having an immediate impact on individuals and NATO facilities.

"If Russia pursues cyberattacks against our firms, our critical infrastructure, we're prepared to take action," Biden said, noting that the government is working along with businesses "to strengthen their cybersecurity security" in order to "sharpen our capability to counter Russian attacks on our cyberspace."

What else can trigger Article 5?

Article 5 could be activated by an intention to carry out a Russian attack as well as an accidental attack against the territory of a NATO member. If it's a deliberate attack certain intelligence analysts are focusing their attention on the Baltics which are countries that don't border Ukraine but were member of the defunct Soviet union that Russians might attempt to seize. The eastern part of the alliance is generally regarded as at the forefront of any war with Russia and this has prompted NATO countries to focus on the strengthening of those members specifically. This is why the president Biden has reiterated his United States' commitment to protecting NATO allies, not just those who are on the eastern side in "authorizing the installation of air and ground forces currently located in Europe to the NATO's eastern flank allies, which include Estonia, Latvia, Lithuania, Poland, and Romania." While few believe Putin has plans to extend his influence beyond Ukraine currently These countries seem to be aware of the threat Russia's recent actions have created. Since the Russian invasion started and they've been among the few countries who have used Article 4 - another provision of the treaty which allows members to submit security issues to the alliance for consideration, which could act as a prelude to Article 5. A further deliberate attack could see Russia contesting Turkey and has shut down two important passageways for warships including both the Bosporus as well as the Dardanelles due to Ukrainian Government pressure. Experts have also identified missile attacks on NATO nations, both they are intentional or unintentional, as being actions which might be triggering Article 5, given that Russia has fired hundreds of missiles against Ukraine since the beginning of the invasion. Experts are keeping an eye monitoring the western border of Ukraine with Poland and Poland, as Ukrainian forces that are retreating to Poland may be attacked by Russians which could lead to the invoke to invoke Article 5. But, if the fighting in eastern and central Ukraine persists, the possibility is less likely.

A Retrospective in Time Learnings from 1962 Cuban Missile Crisis

The threats from Russia towards the United States-led NATO take a scary direction, as Moscow issuing a nuclear warning. This marks the third time the world has been worried about nuclear conflict. As the war begins it's sixth day, the 1st of March 2022 and the Russian military attack on Ukraine increases Putin's rhetoric has grown more and more loud. The Russian president

Vladimir Putin has placed his country on alert for nuclear proliferation, causing fury and demonizing his allies, the United States and its allies. Intelligence and defense experts say that Putin's nuclear debating has caused the world to remember that 1962 "Cuban Missile Crisis." It ran from October 16 until October 28 and was waged by the ex Soviet Union and the United States. The world had never before was so close to nuclear war that could threaten humanity as a whole. The 13 days of tension were among the toughest tests for the leadership of both sides.

In the past 60 years, following 60 years after the Cuban ballistic missile war, the conflict between Russia and Ukraine has rapidly escalated into a significant geopolitical conflict, which has led to Vladimir Putin activating his nuclear arsenal, causing a lot of concern all over the world. It will be interesting to see if Putin and the United States-led NATO will be able to handle the crisis and prevent tensions between the two countries from spiralling into chaos. But there is an important lesson to learn from the standoff of 13 days that erupted between Soviet Union and the United States that eventually ended in the dissolution of cloud of war thanks to the tenacious diplomacy and the exchange of letters between both leaders. The war began with it was discovered that the Soviet Union stationed nuclear-armed missiles in Cuba located close to 90 miles off along the coastline of Florida. Fidel Castro the Cuban revolutionary leader of leftists was a survivor of an American-backed attack during the Bay of Pigs a year prior to. He sought military assistance through the Soviet Union. Nikita Khrushchev who was the Soviet Union's leader recognized a strategic opportunity in Castro's proposal and swiftly set up nuclear missiles of medium range which could strike Washington, DC. United States capital, Washington, DC. Nikita Khrushchev is believed underestimated the seriousness of United States reaction when he declared that he would protect Cuba. After finding out about the Soviet Union's missile delivery towards Cuba and the establishment of military facilities in Cuba with the help of Soviet experts, US President John F.

Kennedy announced the establishment of a naval blockade around Cuba on July 22, 1962. President Kennedy advised the American people of the existence of Soviet missiles and announced a naval blockade in Cuba in a TV address on the 22nd of October. President Kennedy advised the American people of the existence of Soviet missiles and announced a naval blockade in Cuba in a TV address on the 22nd of October. On the same day president Kennedy sent a letter to US president addressed a letter to Khrushchev who was one of the founding Secretary's of the Communist Party of the Soviet Union between 1953 and 1964, stating that the country would not permit assault weapons be sent to Cuba. Additionally, president demanded that his Soviet Union dismantle the missile bases and return the missiles. The letter provoked a heated discussion between the two heads. In the meantime, Washington used the time to keep its forces on alert throughout the world. It was preparing four of its air squadrons to launch air strikes on Cuba and designated areas for missiles, airfields ports, and factories for weapons as targets. The military also mobilized thousands of troops and placed them in Florida in anticipation of the possibility of an military invasion in Cuba. It was also reported that the US Navy sent 180 ships to the Caribbean for an amphibious mission that included more than 40,000 marines along with B-52 bombers armed equipped with nuclear weaponry (B-52 Stratofortress was an American long-range, subsonic nuclear-powered bomber.)

In the course of the negotiations in the course of the talks, participants discussed how the Soviet leader initially did not acknowledge the existence that missiles were in Cuba and claimed that the US naval blockade an "act that is a war crime." In the end, common sense won out. Kennedy and Khrushchev came to an agreement. Since Soviet zones were within the of their range and within range, Khrushchev and Kennedy agreed that the Soviet Union requested that the US eliminate their Jupiter missiles out of Turkey. Khrushchev was willing to take down Soviet missiles that were in Cuba for a fee. Washington has also said they would no longer attack Cuba. Even though diplomacy prevented a major nuclear conflict however, the Soviets tried to present the ending of Cuban Missile Crisis as a victory. But it ended up resulting in Khrushchev's demise as a political figure. Despite the failure of his attempt to lead an attack on The Bay of Pigs, Kennedy's popularity shot up because of his stern stance against the Soviets. The tragic event is a lasting impact upon those in American public. The tragedy was a wake-up call to the world regarding the dangers of nuclear war. It also set the stage for the creation of a Moscow-Washington hotline, and the signing of a treaty that prohibited nuclear tests conducted from The United States, the Soviet Union and the United Kingdom in August 1963. The agreement was shattered in the end, when John F. Kennedy, the President of America John F. Kennedy simultaneously allowed a major weapons buildup that led to the expansion in the US nuke arsenal. In during the Cold War, the maneuver provided US military US the military an edge over the Soviets.

What is the REACTION of the West Russia's actions?

The United States and its European partners have unleashed a series of financial sanctions against Russia which is the most severe ever inflicted on the country's major monetary power including an American sanctions against Russian imports of oil. With an economy that is among the top dozen economies in the world and the speed at that they were implemented was remarkable. The consequences are so extreme that the finance minister of France Bruno Le Maire, referred to them as an "all-out financial and economic conflict," a candid and potentially explosive remark which he swiftly retracted. The sanctions that target Russia's global banking system, the influential people wealthy individuals, as well as Russian fossil fuels are intended to punish the president Putin and those who rely and support Putin, and to crush Russia's economy. Russian economy. It makes conducting commercial activities in Russia difficult. In the short term it is a sign of a serious slowdown in the economy. Since the war of the Russian army, the Russian market for stocks has been shut down, and numerous Russian companies with shares that are that are listed abroad have had their equity values almost eliminated. In the long run, Russian currency has been plummeting since the outbreak of war and sanctions were imposed and is nearing an all-time low. Because around eighty percent (85 percent) of trade between countries is carried out using USD. United states Dollar (USD) and then eventually under US laws sanctions are an essential tool for foreign policy that is in the hands of America. Sanctions are frequently referred as the "first alternative of US international policy" within Washington, DC, according to the sanctions researcher Edoardo Saravalle. "To to emphasize a little the importance of sanctions, the rules that govern those who govern the American banking system is the rules of the world economic system." Saravalle stated. "And Washington could utilize it to use it as an instrument." As the global economy becomes more interconnected and globalized, the US capacity to oversee global commerce via its US currency system has become more powerful. As a result of globalization, huge amounts of exchange and commerce around the world is monitored and controlled in the hands of Washington and its allies across Europe. In the past it has become clear that over time, the United States has also built an effective regulatory system which is led by the Executive Branch to effectively regulate these chokepoints. In the end, any sanctions policy that the US implements is likely to be implemented swiftly and efficiently. In the present, Russia is beginning to be feeling the negative effects of those chokepoints being set aside from US and its allies. United States and its allies particularly in Europe However, the force that sanctions have is American in the sense that United States can even act against the interests of its supposed allies like the President Trump administration do to Iran after pulling off of the nuclear agreement and not leaving the the world without recourse.

Additional sanctions against Russia The US has also imposed regulations that prohibit corporations from supplying a range of products to Russia including aviation parts and components, defense and shipping parts and other high-tech items like communications equipment and semiconductors. These US export restrictions are intended to make it harder for Russia to acquire the items it needs to fight in a long-term war, however they also aim to block vital manufacturing as well as other economic activities that aren't directly connected to war efforts, for example, the commercial airline industry, that is not likely to be able to procure parts to repair its aircraft. Also, there is a complete restriction on US companies supplying gear for Russian military. Russian military. It is also a complete ban on sending equipment to the Russian military. United States has also taken hard measures that seemed unimaginable prior to it: in the Biden administration has banned any import of natural gas as well as coal, oil and in the US. However, the Europeans has not joined with the US in this decision due to the fact that it is exclusively relying upon Russian oil imports for energy, and doesn't have an alternative that it can use, as it said. United Kingdom announced shortly after the United States made public decision of ending Russian energy imports at the closing this year.

In addition, numerous large multinational companies have decided to end commercial ties with Russia as part of what experts in sanctions describe as "overcompliance" It is no legal obligation for firms to end relationships to them or their Russian colleagues, but the CEOs have decided that doing business with Russia isn't worth the risk of reputation or the complexity of operations. Visa and Mastercard for example, have pulled out of operations in Russia. Maersk is one of the largest shipping companies has been forced to suspend Russian reservations. ExxonMobil has pulled out of an enormous gas and oil transaction in Russia and announced that it is not planning any new investments in Russia. BP is an British firm that is listed as the biggest foreign investors in Russia is selling its 19.75 percent stake in Rosneft the Russian oil company with its headquarters in Moscow which has the cost of $25 billion . In addition, Shell is cutting its ties to Gazprom (a Russian majority-owned transnational energy company that is based within the city of Saint Petersburg's Lakhta Center). A long and expanding list of foreign companies refusing to conduct business with a sanctioned country is not uncommon -- Western companies have also halted relations with Iran for instancehowever, like the sanctions the fact that it is happening in a matter of short periods of time rather than years and occurs to the 11th largest economy in the world is unique. The circumstances which led to the company's withdrawal shed insight into one of the main reasons US sanctions could be especially severe: No major Western company is able to afford doing business with a sanctioned nation even if it is permitted by the regulations of sanctions. In the corporate sense there is the "reputational threat" is too significant.

Economic IMPLICATIONS of these sanctions on RUSSIA:

In the coming months and weeks to come, Russian businesses will have adapt their operations to the demands of a shrinking economy , and come up with new ways to run their business within the new limitations they are facing. The Russian economy will shrink by 35% during 2020's second quarter and by 7% over the course of. In general the US bank projects the consequences that sanctions have on the Russian economy will be similar to the declines experienced during the 2008 financial meltdown or the Covid-19 crisis. Russia is also facing other issues, including the escalating withdrawal of businesses from its economy. This shows the unwillingness of CEOs to go over the red line of sanctions. And, unlike other crisis, the rest of the world isn't acting together to penalize Russia economically, believing that war against Ukraine will eventually be too costly and pointless that Putin will seek to negotiate an ending to his war. The sanctions are aimed at achieving a specific objective. The punishments are aimed at a specific goal. State of the Union speech the Joe Biden, President of the United States Joe Biden declared, "We are inflicting pain upon Russia as we stand with the Ukraine's citizens." Ukraine." "Putin is more removed from the world than ever before." . "It is not difficult to imagine that such a drastic stop can't last however, economically weakened economies may be able to continue with a deteriorated condition for a prolonged period of period," says Cornell professor and sanctions expert Nicholas Mulder. In order to actually function as a tool to bring this towards a resolution, Western leaders must "promptly establish clear guidelines to withdraw sanctions in order to call for de-escalation and an end to this devastating dispute," he said. It's not clear what outcome would be considered adequate to end the punishments, be it they're the official kind or the voluntary efforts by companies which range from Visa mastercard, Visa and McDonald's.

How sanctions work and the reason the digital (crypto) currencies won't be able to defeat them

The sanctions imposed by United States and Europe are separated into two categories that are: financial, which affects the banking system as well as the capital market, as well as economic which impact the entire economy of Russia.

In the realm of finance on the financial front, on the financial front, United States Treasury Department has been able to sanction Russian the President Vladimir Putin and eleven other important Russian officials of the Russian government. Their names were added on the list of Nationals Specially Designated which includes drug cartel bosses, as well as officials from countries such those of North Korea, Iran, and Venezuela. The inclusion on the list means that any assets within the global financial system are being frozen in addition, Americans are legally barred from conducting business with those people. A number of Russian Oligarchs also face sanctions and authorities from the US Justice Department and certain European law enforcement agencies are seeking to confiscate billionaires' assets that are not financial, such as yachts and real estate. The individuals and the corporations who they employ to hold assets aren't protected from financial limitations. In addition, the United States has also sanctioned the central bank of Russia and "immobilized" its reserves that it held within the US financial system.

Similar sanctions were also imposed from the European Union, making it difficult for Russia to use the reserves of $630 billion to help prop up the ruble, such as through selling US euros or dollars, and buying the currency of its country, or making purchases to aid in the efforts of the war. The US also banned Russia's biggest banking institution Sberbank that controls a third of Russia's financial assets and from accessing its place in the US bank system. The bank froze all assets owned through VTB Bank, Russia's second-largest bank, which holds one fifth of the country's assets within the US financial system, and barred Americans from conducting transactions with the bank. Russian state-owned enterprises, like Sberbank and Gazprom which is the gas and oil group, are banned from being able to access US equity and bond markets. The exclusion of the banking industry from SWIFT which is the primary messaging system in the global banking system has attracted the most focus from European Union, with US backing. Because of its significance, SWIFT (named after the Belgian organisation that manages it, called the

Society for Worldwide Interbank Financial Telecommunication) is often mistaken for the banking system as a whole. It is actually the system for electronic messaging which is used to send and receive cross-border payment instruction among banks and not the individual bank accounts. Although Russia has tried to set up an alternative method to reduce the effects of precisely this kind of penalty, it's not widely used. SWIFT is utilized by more than 11,000 banks and was utilized in about 70% of all transactions in Russia.

Energy is, however is a significant problem of this regard. It is a major omission in SWIFT sanctions, which were chiseled out because of necessity. In the case of natural gas, Europe is dependent on Russia. As per the International Energy Agency, the European Union purchased 155 billion cubic meters of gas from Russia in 2013 which is roughly 40 percent of its natural gas consumption. Europe can't operate its power stations or heat their homes without Russian gas and pipelines that carry it west haven't been shut down. In fact, the amount of gas that is transported through Russia across Ukraine towards Western Europe surged on the first day of the war. Of course, somebody has be able to purchase the gas, and another person must accept the cash to allow it to flow. This is why the central bank of Russia, Sberbank along with Gazprom's financial division are not subject to the SWIFT ban since they are the primary Russian institutions that receive gas payments from Europe There is no legal mechanism that would prevent the use of SWIFT for anything other than gas payment like. It is the Swiss government, specifically has announced that it will drop its neutrality for a long time and be a part of the sanctions by removing Russian assets that include bank accounts. The most popular bitcoin cryptocurrency was invented to enable individuals who are not able to identify themselves to pay direct without concern for government intervention, so getting around those sanctions which have hampered conventional Russian banking system could be thought to be the point at which the digital currency (crypto) were created to satisfy.

Is it possible for the RUSSIAN Economy to thrive on CRYPTO ON ITS OWN?

It's not even possible. One reason is the value of the cryptocurrency market worldwide currently at $2 trillion and bitcoin is worth just over $800 billion. It's nothing compared to Russia's $630 billion foreign reserves which the Russian government is barred from using within this Western banking system. When it comes to using crypto to avoid the wide-ranging sanctions on a country the size of Russia's, Lloyd Blankfein, the former CEO of Goldman Sachs, put it simply, "there isn't enough now and it's not sufficiently liquid." The problem for Russia's central bank isn't an insufficient amount of money; more, it's an inability to make use of the money that it does have. Since those assets of currency are in lock-up regardless of whether Russia would like to do something crazy, such as acquire all bitcoins in the world however, it won't be able to achieve it. Russia cannot purchase significant crypto currencies due to the same reason that it is in a position to not sell dollars and purchase rubles. This means that it cannot buy and sell any item. For

Russia the sanctions inflicted by the US as well as other nations are wide that attempting to work around the sanctions to prevent a permanent economic collapse is nearly impossible.

A significant academic paper by Henry Farrell and Abraham Newman in the year 2019 claimed that years of globalization in the economy have increased the effectiveness of sanctions due to the fact that "some countries, most notably the United States are able to remove entire businesses or countries from these global networks with significant economic implications." When the study was released in the year 2019, they suggested the possibility that "proper access to the global market requires the ability to connect with global systems, such for those of the US Dollar clearing network as well as SWIFT. SWIFT bank network." We live in a global economy which is interconnected, however the connections are not symmetrical." Also, in terms of the alternatives for Russia are bleak. An effort to enhance economic and financial relations with China could be feasible considering that both countries previously had lower levels of business relations as Iran and China were prior to the time that Iran was recently targeted by the US This shift could have a significant opportunity for development. The growth in commerce between Russia and China is not going to be enough to make up for American or European sanctions. Therefore Russia's economy is likely to shrink as it fights war as Europe and the US and Europe clearly relying on sanctions to lure Russia's president Vladimir Putin into talks to reduce some of the economic burden.

Diplomatic solution

There could, in spite of everything an option for a diplomatic solution? Perhaps "The guns are arguing this moment, but the path of debate must remain fluid," said UN Secretary General Antonio Guterres. It is clear that the discussion continues. It is clear that President Macron of France called the President Putin from Russia. Diplomatic sources confirm that feelers have been delivered to Moscow. Unexpectedly,

Russian and Ukrainian officials have had a meeting to discuss the border with Belarus. They may not have made significant progress. But, in announcing the talks, Putin appears to have accepted the concept of a truce that was negotiated. The question will be whether or not the West is able to offer what diplomats refer to as an "off ramp" (an American word for the exit of the main freeway). Diplomats believe it is crucial to ensure that the Russian president comprehends what is required for Western sanctions to go away to allow a face-saving solution to be feasible. If this is the case, Russia loses the war. Sanctions are beginning to irritate Moscow. As the corpses are brought at home, the opposition grows. President Putin is contemplating whether that he has taken on more than he is capable of handling. He is of the opinion that the shame that comes with losing the war more dangerous for his leadership than the shame of winning the war. China comes in and puts the pressure upon Moscow to reach a settlement and threatening to not purchase Russian gas or oil until the situation is remediated. This is why the Russian president Putin is looking for a way to get out. In the meantime, Ukrainian government is witnessing destruction of their country. They have decided that a settlement through a political process could be a better option than a tragic losses of life. Therefore, diplomats become involved and eventually, a solution is found. Ukraine is one example. It has accepted Russian sovereignty over Crimea as well as a part of Donbas. In the response, Putin recognizes Ukrainian independence and Ukraine's right to further strengthen its ties with Europe. This might not be the situation. It's certainly possible that this scenario could be born out of the aftermath of a savage fight.

What about Vladimir Putin? We're prepared for anything that could happen, Putin said as he began his military invasion. What if it resulted in him losing his authority? This may seem like a flimsy idea. But things have changed recent yearsand these issues are now being considered. "It is possible that there could be a regime change in Moscow as it was in Kyiv," stated Professor Sir Lawrence Freedman, Emeritus Professor of

War Studies at Kings College, London. Why would he think this? Maybe President Putin is fighting a gruelling conflict. There are thousands of Russian soldiers are being killed. Economic sanctions are coming into effect. The popularity of Vladimir Putin is declining. Maybe a popular revolt is in the near future. He is able to suppress resistance through Russia's security forces. But this, however, turns in the wrong direction, and many members of Russia's political, military and economic elite protest against him. The West clarifies that in the event that Putin takes a step down to be replaced with a liberal president, Russia will see some sanctions lifted and regular diplomatic relations returned. This may seem plausible at the moment, however, if there's an unjustified coup and Putin is removed. It could be a stretch if those who profited from the policies of President Putin don't trust that he will defend their interests.

Chapter 9: UNDERSTANDING VLADIMIR'S PUTIN

Putin was at one time an KGB (Soviet spy agency) agent. He joined the KGB in the year 1975. The KGB's coaches noticed that 'He did not have a sense of danger'. What might seem to be dangerous to others might not be dangerous to him? They considered this to be a flaw. He admitted the issue through his autobiography. It is now clear by his savage attack in Ukraine. Unafraid to face the consequences. He has displayed this trait since his the age of adolescence. Putin was born to parents who were working class in the month of October in Leningrad. They lived in Soviet style homes where they shared a space with two families. When he was growing up, youngsters tended to play games with no merit and sports, he chose to pursue an art of combat called "Sambo". With the knowledge that the majority of young men longed to be fighter jet pilots or experts in the field, his goal was to be an operative. His first trip to the KGB agency came as teenager. In 1975, he was a graduate of

Leningrad University and went directly to join the KGB in the same year. At the time, was sent into East Germany where he specialised in "Smokes as well as Mirrors'. Before an attack on Georgia and Ukraine the Georgian had an interview where he told of an incident in his college days , when both he and his martial arts instructor were driving through Leningrad and he spotted the truck filled with roughage. When he was driving, he decided to relax and grab some feed into his hand. He then had his instructor advised him" you should be prepared to take risks". He responded "I believed that the smell of the feed was amazing". The story was shared with his supporters. What a politician wouldn't reveal to his supporters. He proudly presents himself as an ogre and an indiscreet. Simply shows what kind of person that he truly is. The memoir was written by him in 2000. Incredibly, he became the into the leader of Russia in the same year. In 1991, he became vice-mayor in Saint Petersburg. The breakup of the Soviet Union caused things to be uncomfortable for him. In 1997, he was appointed as Vice Chief of the Presidential staff. In 1998, he became the chief of the Federal Security Administration, which was the brand new KGB replacement agency. In 1999, he was elected the first Vice-Prime Minister of Russia Then the Prime Minister, and, in 2000, the President was elected. His career took off when Russia's honor dipped because Boris Yeltsin Russia's first President was a drunk and dishonest, and was the subject of ridicule. In addition, he engaged with the West in order to satisfy Putin's wishes. While the Cold War is over, its legacy remains. Putin who was a former KGB agent has struggled to get himself to trust in the West. Putin has never been able to ignore the ways in which NATO "North Atlantic Treaty Organisation is growing and every one of the nations on the list below have turned into a part of the alliance:

The founding Part Nations in 1949 were

Belgium, Canada, Denmark, Iceland, Italy, Luxemburg, Norway, Netherlands, Portugal, Joined Realm and US.

1952 Greece and Turkey,

1955 West Germany,

1982 Spain was a participant in the outbreak war.

1990 Germany,

1999 Czech Republic, Hungary, Poland.

2004 Bulgaria, Estoria, Latvia, Lithuania, Romania, Slovakia, Slovenia.

2009 Albania, Croatia.

2017 Montenegro.

2020 North Macedonia.

In 1999, he was concerned NATO would expand to include ex-Soviet republics, and eventually take over Russia. He was astonished that Yeltsin did not do what was required to control NATO. Putin was looking for the creation of a Russian state that was independent, strong and recognized. Chechnya provided him with the opportunity to build the Russian state.

The region split with Russia in 1991 and gained its own independence. In addition, Chechen rebels had turned into a source of trouble for Russia. The year 1999 saw a series of bomb shootings rocked Russia at Moscow, Buynasksk, and Volgodonsk with the loss of 307 people in the Russian urban areas during the time the Prime Minister was in charge. He began naming, degrading and blaming Chechens on television. He started holding press conferences, stir up nationalist attitudes and make Chechens angry. He promised to stop the terrorists. Thus, his endorsement appraisals went away from the 2% before bombings to 45% after bombings. The speculation at the time were made suggesting that Putin could have faked the blasts in order to boost his ascent to the presidency. The theory was that KGB experts might have fabricated the bombs in order to boost Putin's popularity. Russia rejected this idea and waged war on Chechnya from August 1999 until April 2000. There were 80,000 dead and Chechnya was integrated into Russia again. Boris Yeltsin stepped down from his post as President and appointed Putin as Acting President, on the night of December 31st 1999. Putin is a shrewd character , did not inform his best half before his the day of his appointment as acting President despite having been aware of the appointment for quite a long period of time. In addition, it is reported that the Russian Parliament was unaware about his plan to attack Ukraine also. Despite the fact that he had asked permission for troops to go to uncharted locations, the officials didn't think they would be able to strike Ukraine. In reality, Putin really did not need to get that permission. As the head of the Russian Armed Forces He is free to send troops wherever that he wants. Therefore, going to the parliament can be seen as an act of deceit. In addition, he is a fan of the thrill of stunts. He once swam in the ocean, bringing two objects from the lower portion of the ocean together at the same time. However, it was later discovered that Putin's official spokesperson had admitted that the Greek Urn find was arranged. Putin is featured on the media for fishing, arm wrestling, horse riding, displaying his butterfly swimming skills as well as co-steering a plane , fixing the satellite transmitter to a tiger's neck hunting, etcetera. They show that he's proficient, determined as well as a reliable regulator of facts, and a storyteller who tells his own personal story. Similar to the story of Ukraine. One wayis that Russia is a victim people who were affected by the bomb are casualties , and the recently chosen government of Kiev is filled with Nazists therefore Putin has decided to send troops on a "Denazification Mission'. The building 7 has been destroyed and honest citizens have been murdered due to the fact that Putin believes that Ukraine is one. He believes that Ukraine and Russia are one. Putin will not let anything get in the way of the country he is a part of. He has never read any book written by an Soviet critic. He stated "I do not read books written that contain people who have slapped their country. He is supported by Russia's powerful KGB officials. He has been in the KGB's hands for over 22 years now. He has driven Russia into a few battles. He calmed his critics who questioned him, and he resisted the media. In the last few days several hundred people have been arrested in awe Russians combat Ukraine attack. In 2020, Putin was elected President of Russia for lifetime. In the last 14 years the president has had three fights. He will remain in his position until 2036. He has another 14 years and 13 Soviet Republics left to leave.

UKRAINIAN PRESIDENT, VOLODYMYRZELENSK.

Zelensky became Ukraine's first leader in 2019, after an epic land slide. Zelensky is a vocal opponent of Russia. He is a vocal opponent of Russian control over Eastern Ukraine. 73 percent of Ukraine elect him president in the year 2019. Today Volodymyr Zelensky speaks to the needs of Ukraine that must remain independent of Russia as Vladimir Putin aspires to be the one to revive Russian colonialism.

PUTIN'S COMPLAIN:

The primary reason for Putin's protest to start the war is that NATO following the Cold War should not matter. Furthermore, in the year the year 1990 NATO assured that they did not extend Eastwards in any way, but the majority of former Soviet states were incorporated into NATO. The argument goes that as part of NATO's NATO Security Agreement, an hostile missiles will be deployed in Ukraine. This is on Russians terrace , and poses a direct threat for Russia is Ukraine become an integral part of the EU (European Union) and other social/business groups.

The HISTORY of RUSSIA and UKRAINE dating back to the 9th Century

S

Some time back Kyiv used to be more powerful in the past than Moscow. Additionally, Ukraine and America were engaged in war. In the 9th century there was a nation called Kievan Rus. The Slavic population lived there, as well as the capital city Kiev was their capital city. Between 980 and 1015, The Kievan Rus was ruled by a superb ruler named Volodimer. In Russian the name is Vladimir and in Ukrainian Volodimer, and according to the whims of fate they are those of rulers of these two nations in the present. Russians along with Bella Russians draw their foundations from the Slavic state. There was a lot of difference in the years that followed, and for the majority of time, Ukraine was under Russian rule. In the early 1900s, both were both so successful (Soviet republics). Russia is the most influential among the fifteen Soviet Republics as well as Ukraine the second most powerful among the fifteen Soviet Republics. Ukraine was home to security companies as well as huge agricultural facilities and was the home of a large portion of Soviet Atomic Arms stockpiles. In the Cold War, Ukraine was the subject of the war in the US. It was the time when

Soviet Union disintegrated in 1991. Ukraine gained independence, as did Russia. Ukraine obtained a substantial portion of the armouries of the Atomic Age, that include items:

176 Intercontinental Ballistic Missiles. 1249 Warheads for nuclear. The 66 Strategic bombers. 700 cruise missiles with nuclear-tipped cruise missiles as well as Tactical Nuclear weapons.

Ukraine offered them all the rest to Russia in 1994. In the exchange, Moscow assured Ukraine security. Russia committed to respecting Ukraine's sovereignty. They signed the Budapest Arrangement's reminder, along with Belarus, UK, Kazakhstan, US. In November 2013 Viktor Yanukovych then president of Ukraine was a household name for his insincerity, dishonesty, and being openly supportive of Moscow. He rejected the possibility of an EU Economic accord which might have impliedmore significant Integration with the European/Eastern Union, rather he decided to accept a $15 billion loan from

Russia. To many Ukrainians it was like the country was being sold to Moscow which is why a fight began to break out. EUROMAIDAN which was referred to as. Europe and Maidan Nezalezhnosti, in light of how the dissent focused on Europe and Maidan due to it being that the protesters were at Ukraine's Maidan which is also known as the Independence Square this day. Protesters shouted "sign to the EU agreement' and Yanukovych should step down. Russia stood by Yanukovych as president. Yanukovych and the West stood with the demonstrators. The month of February was when when Yanukovych's government was overthrown, the president was exiled out of Ukraine. Yanukovych fled to Russia and only a small portion of every single Ukrainian were happy about it. Many in Russia's Russian speaking East required Yanukovych to stay. After his removal the majority of people were dissatisfied, while Russia was angry. To avert the crisis, Moscow took over Crimea. The landmass is located on the Black Sea. It was in 1954 that Soviet

Union dealer Nikita Khrushchev, emigrated Crimea away from Russia in Ukraine. The Crimea was transferred by Ukraine by the Ukrainian Communist Republic from the Russian socialist Republic in the belief that Khrushchev believed the deal will strengthen the love between Ukrainians as well as the Russians. Russia along with Crimea were vital to and within the Soviet Union. This is why the exchange wasn't worth much. When Ukraine was made an independent state at the beginning of 1991 Crimea was also part of it. The Landmass was granted a unique independence. It was the home of Russian Army installations as well as Moscow promised to respect Crimea's Independence. However, many within Russia are of the opinion that Crimea should not have been allowed to be a part of Ukraine. In 2014 Yanukovych had to be exiled for fowling in Ukraine. Russian military began to hold onto the government structure in Crimea. Russia slowly began to take over the entire Peninsular. Then on the 16th of March:

Crimeans casted a ballot to become part of Russia 2014. For Putin Crimea, it was Crimea's independence be however and for other nations as well, this was Crimea's inclusion. The main focus in that time went into East Ukraine where Russia backed separatists began to hold onto an area. Furthermore, Ukrainian powers didn't jump into a hostile posture immediately. At the same time. On the 17th of July, 2014. Malaysian plane flight 298 crashed in the vicinity of the rebels. Ukrainian authorities decided to eliminate the rebels. The separatists began losing ground, so the Russian Armed forces came in to attack Eastern Ukraine and battled close by renegades. An ongoing dialogue among Ukraine, Russia and the West was the result. This led to the Minsk agreement of 2014 that was approved in 2014 as 'a ceasefire, withdrawal of military forces races in rebel-held regions' was the future would hold. Ukraine agreed to. Ukraine agreed to allow the holding of rulings in the insurgent controlled regions. In the midst of eight years the Minsk court has not been implemented. Ukraine is still the largest European nation , excluding Russia. With 603,550 Sq Km, with a population of 44 million and a gross domestic product that exceeds $155 billion for each capital payment of $3,727. In the present, Ukraine is divided into the East and West. The West believes it is more European while the East is closer to Russia. In the west, the majority of Ukrainians speak Ukrainian however while however, in East East 33% speak local Russian. While in the West Russia is considered to be untrustworthy, but in the East Russia is seen from the standpoint of shared heritage and history. Ukraine is also in conflict with its forces fighting insurgents in east. The revolutionaries rule Luhansk as well as Donetsk. They are both part of Donetsk and Luhansk, they are known as the Donbas district. The Russian troops are stationed near the Ukrainian border.

WHAT DO PUTIN WANT?

P

utin Putin needs NATO to cease the growing. Ukraine is keen to join NATO and, be that it is, Putin needs NATO to stop Ukraine as well as every previous Sovien state. This is only a small portion of the story , for much is hidden in both the history of the country and its legislation. In the time Putin was in charge of Crimea the rating of his support increased. Around 9/10 Russians were in favor of their leader. In a report, that also includes support for the Ukraine system. A large portion of Ukraine helps Russia by restoring its supreme power status. Through the ages, many Russians consider Ukraine's independence to be an mistake. One of every six Ukrainians is ethnic Russian. 1 out of 3 Ukrainians communicate with Russian as a language spoken in the local area. This means that Putin is right when he states that generally that they were one. But, as you can see the assertion that Ukraine due to the history of its province isn't correct. Past colonialism can't legitimize present day expansionism. It is evident from history the fact that Ukraine had been forcibly degraded following around 1700. Russian chief, Catherine the great, began to search for Ukraine. The ethnic Russian was brought to this part of the planet. Schools were instructed to teach Russian the language. Around 1800 in the 1800s, it was evident that the Ukrainian language was banned. In 1930, Soviet president Joseph Stalin, who Putin's grandfather worked with as cook, caused death toll in Ukraine. A large number of Ukrainians died. The region was then rebuilt with ethnic Tatars relocated and replaced with Russians. This is why Ukraine has been identified with a lot of Russian natives. Russia was always fond of the eastern part of Ukraine due to its cold climate and had abundant grounds as well as iron minerals. The Ukrainian connection to Russia was not involuntary. Putin repeatedly discusses the "Holy Russ'. Putin says "Russians as well as Ukrainians have a common language ".

70 70% Ukrainians are against this notion.

72% of people think of Russia as a state that is antagonistic.

Today, 33.3 percent of Americans are ready to go to war against Russia.

21.7 percent are ready to organize a common opposition against Russia.

67% of people want to join the EU.

59% want to be a part of NATO.

Is the EU to blame the War in UKRAINE?

M anyone can fault anyone else blames the EU in triggering the conflict that has been brewing in Ukraine. Ukraine isn't seen as a legitimate contender for EU participation, but it is important to sign an affiliation agreement with the EU (wherein both parties have agreed to adjust their economies to specific areas and expand their the ties between them in terms of politics) from the year 2017. As part of the affiliation agreement, a comprehensive and extensive International alliance

(DCFTA) 'Deep Comprehensive Free Trade was been applied for temporary use from January of 2016. The EU agrees to provide Ukraine with financial and political assistance, access to information and research as well as access into EU markets. The agreement requires the two parties to move slowly towards a union in line with the EU's regular security and Safeguard strategy as well as European Defence Agency policies. The Russians consider the alliance with Russia as an EU strategy to undermine their power within Eastern Europe. In one way or another, this is true. In any event they reacted with anger that the EU has negotiated the affiliation agreement with Ukraine which is the neighbor which has the most impact to Moscow even though they are in good faith and the fact that the deal could have a major impact to and affect the Russian economy. The Russians might be wrong in this respect. In September 2013, in Northern Russia at a yearly gathering of the Valdai club, Putin said that assuming Ukraine had signed its territory with the

DCFTA "low price and competitive EU products would be flooded into Ukraine as Ukraine will have to sell everything it produces to Russia. Russian market. Additionally, they'd have to protect the Russian marketplace". Putin somehow or other got Yanukovych to not sign a consent form to an EU arrangement. This led to Yanukovych being overthrown and the subsequent taking over of Crimea by Putin. The responsibility which the EU has to fulfill for this complicated affair is not that much as it tried to talk with the Russians regarding its relationship with Ukraine but the Russians weren't interested until after negotiations had began. The bi-annual summit between the EU and Russia the commission usually formulated the finalizations on the plan. Igor Yurgens, a senior advisor to the the then Russian President Dmitri Medvedev, reviews at these summits, the commission's

Jose Manuel Barroso, has asked Jose' Manuel Barroso, president of the European Commission, to invite Russians to negotiate the agreement. However Barroso's Russians weren't keen on discussing the agreement. At that time, Russia was not averse to Kyiv's relationship with the EU. Vladimir Putin had even said in 2004 that Russia would welcome Ukraine's inclusion in the EU. Despite the fact that NATO clearly was a different matter. Each of these was changed after Putin returned in his Russian government in the year 2012 to serve a third term. He was determined to transform the customs associations that linked Belarus, Kazakhstan and Russia into a more exciting "Eurasian Economic Union" (EEU) which he believed to become a crucial stabilizing force for the EU. Additionally, he desired Ukraine to be able to lend the project credibility and weight. Unexpectedly, after the agreement was ratified in May and March 2014 and May 2014, the EU attempted to keep Russians interested and informed. In September 2014, under Russian tensions, Ukraine president Petro Poroshenko announced that he would not delay the implementation of Ukraine's part to the DCFTA. The EU recognized this and agreed to the Russian request that officials from both the EU, Ukraine and Russia regularly meet to discuss the impact of the agreement on Russia and the steps that can be taken to minimize any adverse effects. After these gatherings, EU officials concluded that the DCFTA had no effect to the Russian economy, as the agreements would not prevent or alter exchange between Ukraine or Russia. The EU did not accept Russia's request for it to be granted permission to alter parts of the DCFTA in the belief that Ukraine is a sovereign nation which had to conduct its own negotiations to the EU. Russia continued to warn of disastrous economic outcomes, unless Ukraine had to destroy the DCFTA. When Ukraine finally signed the agreement, in January it was clear that there was nothing more financial damage that Moscow could inflict and it was able to eliminated the bulk of its trade with Ukraine. (In the April election that year, the Dutch cast a vote against the affiliation plan but, despite that, EU leaders are probably likely to come up with a solution to save its majority). The long-winded conclusion to this question is the EU should be punished for not examining the fundamental results of its plans regarding Ukraine. The government's public perception was that Russia might react to eastern association (Ukraine dilemma). However that the EU's inability predict Russia's behavior does not make it liable for their actions.

WHO CAN BLAME 'NATO' or RUSSIA who is it?

T

Here are the different perspectives to every there are many sides to each. Consider each side prior to making an assessment or a conclusion. On one hand is NATO which has been dictating the world's story. On the other side is Russia seen as the monster. In spite of the fact that there is a compelling argument in favor of Russia. The story also has a different perspective. What was the motive that brought people to the point of the invasion? In spite of the fact the kind of thing Putin did is not common. The leaders in Moscow claim they are the irritated party and the survivors of NATO and are acting on good reasons. For the last 25 years NATO has been scurrying across Russia's borders, and the previous Soviet states have become its allies. NATO collusion with the military has sucked all the security belts of Moscow. Russia is adamant that this move could constitute an incitement. This is a threat to their security and will not be a good thing for both parties. The notice of advance was clear, but NATO did not take it seriously due to their lack of shrewdness or arrogance. In the end, Moscow's interests were ignored and continued to extend the agreement until the situation exploded in Ukraine. Was NATO force Ukraine into this war? NATO can be described as a partnership that is a security alliance between America in the United States and Europe. It is a part of the conflict. The shape was created following World War II. It was aimed at securing 'Democratic Freedom". 4 April 1949, The North Atlantic deal was agreed on. It was a defamation of Soviet agreement, and was aimed at combating any future hostility from the USSR. It outlined a different overall influence over Europe and ensured all people total security. A set of guidelines in the 5th section in the NATO agreement requires the members to defend each other in the event of conflict. It states that "A committed assault on one or more members in Europe or North America will be viewed as an assault on all of them". This allowed NATO partners to create a security measures. It was a co-operation of nations that were liberal. A force for democratization that will promote normal characteristics and values, and also stand against the rise of socialism. Thus, Moscow saw this alliance as be a threat to its advantages. In turn, Russia birthed the Warsaw agreement in 1952 in order to alternative to NATO that included East

Germany, Poland, Bulgaria, Romania, Hungary, Russia and Czechoslovakia.

There were five motives the reasons why this treaty was ratified.

Five Attacks:1. 1610-1612 Polish living in Kremlin. 2. The Swedish invasion of Russia in the early 18th century.3. The Napoleonic invasion in Russia in 1812, and the second world wars. 4. 1914-1918: coalition versus partners. 5. Germany and the Nazi attack on the Soviet Union in 1941 in each instance and the Russian state was destroyed. The fear of the West was deeply rooted in Russia. Moscow began to view NATO as a study of American expansionism. The assessment was not entirely wrong. 1989 Berlin wall collapsed. The 1991 Soviet Union deteriorated and the iron drapery was destroyed. Europe command was centered around one question "Should Germany get attached to NATO along with the US or join the Warsaw agreement together with Russia?" US government in 1990 under George W Bush made a suggestion to

Russia. If Germany became an NATO member, NATO would quit growing and not even move 1 inch to the east. The new partners would not be able to join. In the present, US claims it has not made promise in any way several memos and other records taken from US documents prove that it was not the case. In any event, Moscow accepted the proposition and smashed the Warsaw accord with the belief that the West would do the similar. It was believed that NATO is too much would be dissolved regardless, NATO wouldn't stop operations and was open to new members. Russia thought it was as a betrayal, and NATO continued to make the deeper into the blade stretching eastwards to 2017. And into 2020. In 2021, Russia found three more aspirants specifically: Bosnia and Herzegovina, Georgia and Ukraine. NATO is also in talks in talks with Finland, Serbia and Sweden. Thus, most of East Europe which used to be crucial for an Soviet Union has now joined NATO regardless of Russia's notice in advance. The most warmly agreed-to admonition was made in 2007 when Putin was present at the annual Munich gathering. Putin said "NATO has placed its cutting edge power on our line. This incident is an actual threat to the integrity of trust among the people. We have the right to ask who is the target of this change is being viewed? What was the result of the assertions our western counterparts offered following the demise of the Warsaw agreement? ". These opinions have been amplified by the majority from American tacticians.

On June 26, 1997 50 notable international strategy experts, which included former legislators, military officials, negotiators , and academicians signed and wrote an unofficial letter addressed to the President Clinton showing their opposition towards NATO extension. The letter was deemed to be a " Strategy error of notable proportions'.

George Kenan the father of America's strategy. A chronologist and ambassador said about NATO "I consider it an incredibly mistake. There is no reason for this. There was no evidence of compromising any other person".

The year 2008 was the time that William J Burns past US diplomat to Russia wrote addressed to the US state division, stating "Ukrainian part of NATO is one of the most exciting of potential redlines to the Russian world-class. From the barbarians hiding in the shadows to Moscow's Kremlin as well as Putin's determined anti-liberal defenders at home I'm unable to locate anyone who regards Ukraine joining NATO as more than an immediate test for Russian interest".

Robert N Gates, the defense secretary under the Bush and Obama's government, stated that "attempting to incorporate Georgia as well as Ukraine in NATO was actually overstepping. This was an example of ignoring the fact that Russians were thinking about their own important diplomatic strategy".

According to his diary, Strobe Talbot, a former US Secretary of State stated

"Numerous Russians consider NATO to be a legacy of Cold War. They state that they've broken up the Warsaw Pact and wonder why the West hasn't done the same ".

However, successive American presidents did not give any notification to these alerts, and continued to expand NATO. The idea of integrating a country that is within Russian's border into a coalition that is not familiar to them is an act of incitement. Ukraine is an independent country and is entitled to be a part of NATO however, how will this be beneficial to NATO? Why did they insist on it? They completely ignored the long-running conflict that exists between NATO as well as Russia. Many Russians are shocked by the decline of their Soviet Union. In just a few minutes they were able to lose 33% their area, half of the population and the power of their military. They became less secure prior to the western cooperation. They believed that a corrupt arrangement was forced upon them, and that at the time they felt more vulnerable and saw any country that left the influence of Russia as a pity and cause for embarrassment. However, all of these do not legitimize the war. Russia's actions are criminal without a doubt. buts , yet the west isn't completely innocent in the same way. They didn't take the actions they could have done to prevent this war.

What is the reason why Russia has ANNEXed CRIMEA?

O

investigators at experts in the field of investigation at a European gasoline conference gave an extended presentation entitled "Is the Black Sea the new North Sea?". The report referred to topographical studies that identified that the Black Sea waters around Ukraine as with "enormous prospect of exploration" However, they viewed the Russian region as less attractive. On August 12, 2012 Ukraine signed an official agreement with an Exxon-led group to pull out gas and oil in Ukrainian's Black Sea waters. The Exxon group had beat Lukoil the Russian group. The acquisition to Crimea by Russia signified that Russia had taken control of the Crimean part of Ukraine's public gas company within a matter of seconds, offering Russia exploratory material regarding the Black Sea. Russia was able to acquire Crimean landmass, and an oceanic zone several times its size , with the ability to submerge assets worth billions of dollars. Russia claimed the acquisition was a an opportunity to regain its rightful domain, while not focusing on the rush to extract gas and oil which has caused warming of the Black Sea. The move extended the boundaries of Russia's oceans, quietly providing Russia the right to control huge gas and oil resources while fighting a massive loss for Ukraine's hopes of energy autonomy. Russia took this action under an international agreement that grants nations the power to control regions that extend that extend up to 230 miles from their coasts. The country had tried unsuccessfully to gain access to energy resources in the same area in a settlement made that it reached with Ukraine two years ago. In the present, Russia has constructed a $4 billion flyover that connects it to the central region and is currently trying to link up the confiscated areas in the south Ukraine via Mariupol. There are also massive gas stations within the east Donbas district. Putin does not need Ukraine as a direct competitor close to home , supplying energy to the West with energy sources, as this could hurt Russia's economy.

RUSSIA SANCTION:

Ukraine as well as a number of other countries protested against the acquisition of Crimea by Russia and believed it's an infringement of international law and Russian agreed agreements to defend the honor of the region of Ukraine which include the 1991 Belavezha agreement that outlined an agreement on the Common Wealth of Independent states and The 1975 Helsinki Accords, the 1994 Budapest memorandum of security guarantee and the 1997 settlement on the kinship, collaboration and cooperation with Ukraine and the Russian Confederacy as well as Ukraine. The result was Russia being hit with a succession of sanctions across the world from various countries, EU, Worldwide associations. Russia also responded with sanctions against a variety of nations and the absolute ban on imports of food coming from Australia, Canada, Norway, Japan, US and the Europeans Union. The sanctions aggravated the collapse of Russian rule and also the Russian economic emergency. According to Ukrainian officials, these sanctions forced Russia to alter its policy toward Ukraine and reduced Russian military's advance within the district. Spokespersons from the countries who were penalized Russia declare that they'll lift sanctions on Russia only when Moscow meets all of the Minsk II arrangements.

What drives PUTIN's:

There are a variety of speculations. Putin is believed to be seeking to restore an Russian power-base and sphere throughout Eastern Europe, chiefly embracing the former Soviet Republics, including currently self-governing Estoria, Latvia, Lithuania, Belarus, Georgia and Ukraine. He's often been vocal about their "loss" following the demise of the Soviet Union. Putin could also be looking to demonstrate to the West and Russians that the country is not yet an absolute power.

What is the reason for UKRAINE?

Putin worries about the tactical significance Ukraine which, as the country's southern flank. It is now adjusting to the west. Putin is concerned about the growing closeness of Kyiv to NATO. He is also opposed to Kyiv's expanding connection to the EU. The worst part is that according to him, Ukraine is a vote based system (autonomy) which is characterized by freedom of speech and a free media that is able to vote without reservation for its the leaders. In the end, Russians have no such chances. If they had, Putin would not last for long as president. In addition, Putin is a nostalgic revisionist who regards Ukraine as an integral part of the history of Russia and also as an emblem of the Cold War's defeat for Russia.

What is the reason why PUTIN has to be STRUCKED now?

R

A study has shown that Russia's assertion that a war against Ukraine under Zelensky's leadership will have minimal impact could be correct. Volodymr Zelensky, the 44-year older president from Ukraine was a former actor who won more than 70% of votes in Ukraine's 2019 presidential election based on the power of an online video praising corruption is not experienced in administration. His administration, which is dominated by actors from his past are also not experienced in the field of the management of. He was unable to put his troops in defensive positions, nor start formulating strategies to protect his troops should an attack be launched on their country by Russia despite all the Russian's previous threats and the evidence upon the walls. To display their inexperience, inadequacy and lack of preparation to defend their citizens The defence ministry has urged people to launch Molotov cocktail (petrol bombs) at Russian tank soldiers with explosive weapons. It's similar to entering combat with the toothpick. Putin knew this as well, in addition to the reality that Ukraine was not yet integrated into NATO. Putin was also aware of Western inefficiencies. NATO was humiliated during the year of Afghanistan in Afghanistan. Joe Biden who crusaded to stop wars and not be involved in new wars , has altered America's strategy for international engagement and its military assets to China and not Europe. Over the last two decades, when America's military was busy fighting in Iraq, Libya and Afghanistan, Russia was silently building her economy, arsenal and acquiring technology that was not even thought of 20 years before. He has redesigned the Russian military and has modernized and expanded the nuclear arsenal of Russia, rehabilitated and expanded Russian intelligence agencies and activities and has taken over Russia's media releases and integrated state-owned industries and eliminated opposition from the United Russia party. This has left the West with sanctions as their sole alternative. This is fast becoming a blunt weapon due to the fact that Russia is home to more than $600bn of reserves on the international stage, an enormous storage of oil and gas as well as access to the second-largest economy , China's market, and an exploding arms trade with India and gas exports to Europe. This is the reason Zelensky sought out the West to stop Russian acces to swift policy that allows banking transactions, as well as to freeze Russian Central Bank accounts that are located in the West including the assets of Putin and stop purchasing Russian gas and oil. It is believed that Putin must win a major victory to secure his nation's support, discredit his anti-western policies and excuse the system's degraded state and justify the challenges Russians have to face as a result of the western sanctions imposed on Russia following the first of his attacks upon Ukraine in 2014. In 2014, Putin seized Crimea and took over Eastern Donbas district. Putin might also want to demonstrate to the west, Ukraine as well as Russians that Russia is still an absolute power.

Chapter 10: Conflicts Impacts on economies

What will the effects of war be on the Market

The dispute in the region between Russia as well as Ukraine is a huge issue for investors. It is reported that the US along with Europe are considering sanctions against Russia as a response to the invasion of Crimea which raises the prospect of an economic war. If this turns into a gun battle and the results could be devastating.

It's not only stocks that are in danger in this case. As tensions escalate the oil price could increase even more and currencies could be affected, too.

Here's what you must know about the conflict , and how it might impact your assets.

Stocks

The stock market has proved exceptionally resilient to geopolitical tensions in the last few years. Investors have been obsessed with the Federal Reserve's policy on monetary policy that they've neglected everything elsehowever, that could be changed at any moment.

Over the past several days, Russian stocks have declined by 5%, whereas American stocks have increased by 4percent. It's not a huge difference when you consider the issues we're facing this time, but it's something to keep in mind.

The ongoing conflict in Ukraine and Russia Russia and Ukraine could hurt investors' confidence across the region, which includes Russia.

"The Russian market has been in a state of flux since the conflict began," said Sebastien Barbe the head of emerging markets studies for Credit Agricole. "It's not just about Russia but also Ukraine as well as the other countries in the region."

But experts say the effect could be more severe in the event of sanctions being imposed on Russia. The situation is relatively stable and if tensions rise further, it could impact markets more.

"Markets are typically extremely resilient and will react with a knee-jerk response when events go south However, they can recover very swiftly," Barbe said.

Russian shares have dropped more than 10 percent of their value this year, and the ruble has weakened to the US dollar. The currency has fallen almost 7% against the greenback in the first quarter of 2014.

"We think this is the worst negative event to Russian asset prices since 1998" declared William Jackson the emerging market economics expert working at Capital Economics. The crisis in the ruble of 1998 resulted in a dramatic decline in the value of Russian currency, and a default on the government's debt.

The central bank of Russia raised interest rates on Tuesday in order to halt an upswing in prices which caused the ruble to fall to new lows against the euro and the dollar.

As the Ukraine crisis escalates as the Ukraine conflict escalates, the Kremlin is becoming more worried about the possibility that Western sanctions on financial transactions could be imposed against Russia.

There are concerns that this could trigger an exodus of capital from the country, leading to the collapse of the rouble and massive inflation.

As if that weren't enough, Russia's economy is already in the process of slowing down and could be headed towards a recession.

What effect would financial sanctions impact?

"The probable scenario for sanctions will be implemented within a few weeks," says Anders Aslund who was a former economic advisor of the Russian president and now a senior researcher in the Peterson Institute for International Economics in Washington.

"Those are likely to freeze certain accounts of Russian businesses and individuals who are who are enrolled in Western banking institutions."

The war began when Russia acquired Crimea in 2014. Crimea area in the year 2014 and it has continued to rage in the eastern region of Ukraine. Separatists from Russia have been combating the Ukrainian army and are backed by NATO.

The economy of Russia is currently being hit by international sanctions due to its involvement during the Ukraine crisis. The currency of the country, the rouble, has dropped around 50 percent against the dollar this year. It was on the news Tuesday that it sank to the record minimum that was 65.5 per dollar. It is also the Russian stock market has also plunged.

The situation was further deteriorated as Malaysia Airlines flight MH17 was destroyed by rebels in a region in the eastern part of Ukraine. The plane's 298 passengers were killed, including two-thirds of them Dutch citizens.

Western nations are accusing pro-Russian militants shooting down the plane using missiles supplied by Russia However,

Moscow has denied that it was involved in the shooting.

Russian Vladimir Putin, the Russian president Vladimir Putin said he hoped that "common sense" prevailed and the international relationship would not be sacrificed to "confrontational goals".

The Deputy Prime Minister of Russia Dmitry Rogozin said that Moscow might consider limiting flights over Siberia in Europe and Asia since it will no longer be able to ensure their security within Ukrainian airspace if they continue to fly over Russian territories.

Following the announcement that Russian the president Vladimir Putin signed a decree that recognized Crimea as an independent state and the U.S. is responding with sanctions on individuals and organizations that are located in Russia. In addition, the European Union is also imposing sanctions against Russia and plans to establish an asset freeze system that could be tied to Russian leaders who are involved in the war.

The current crisis could have economic consequences, primarily on Russia that is under pressure to increase interest rates due to the threat of the flight of capital. However, there is a chance of collateral damage elsewhereas well.

The growth in GDP in Russia is predicted to slow this year, from 2percent last year to just one percent in the opinion of Oxford Economics. The investment bank noted that the conflict could cause individuals and businesses on each side of the war to reduce spending.

"It's not only the impact on companies direct victims of sanctions" claims John Lomax, senior analyst at HSBC Global Research. "If you're an Russian bank or business with dollars in deposits or loans and you're in Russia, it's going be much more difficult to access the dollars." HSBC expects second quarter growth of Russia to be 0.1% as a result.

If the recent actions of Russia in Ukraine were meant to demonstrate to an United States and its European allies that Moscow has the capability and determination to be a significant participant on the global stage, it's possible to conclude the Russian president Vladimir Putin has succeeded.

What he's also done is put at risk his own future and the future of his nation. Through the annexation of Crimea it is forcing Russia into an isolation from the world that has not been experienced since the invasion of the Soviet Union in Afghanistan. In the end it will only harm Russia.

As much as Putin's repressive actions has split the world as well, it has divided Russia itself. While a lot of Russians do agree with his actions as president in Ukraine Others see him as the president as trying to create the old form that is a new form of Russian imperialism.

Conclusion

The idea of a peaceful conflict between Russia and Ukraine was a flimsy idea, because the need to demonstrate its authority through the use of force was a major factor against the majority group in Ukraine. To safeguard their accomplishments in the political arena the Ukrainians began fighting in the Donbas region against the people living there, declaring them as their own citizens. It was just the matter of time until they would have to confront their military rivals, particularly from Russia that wanted exact revenge for its long-running conflict and also to maintain its international status.

Ukraine is an independent country, Russia has troops and tanks on their territory. they have tanks and troops on their territory, the U.S. is no longer supporting the separatists in Kiev as well as The U.S., EU and NATO are not in conflict with Ukraine or Russia, nor are they supporting Russian as well as Ukrainian residents in any manner. Russia has committed a strategic error by interfering in Ukraine and transferring troops to Crimea in order to defend against nazis, but it was done on Ukrainian territory that violated international law. The actions aren't endorsed internationally and therefore they have committed an unlawful act.

President Kyrgyzstan is being Ukrainian leader is loudly decried by Western leaders , but there are indications that Russia is not going to back down. One Russian leader claimed it could cause an "catastrophe" to Russia in the event that Ukraine moves to join NATO and NATO, something Ukraine's acting president has said was one of the goals of his country. We will keep you updated as it unfolds.

www.ingramcontent.com/pod-product-compliance
Lightning Source LLC
Chambersburg PA
CBHW071124130526
44590CB00056B/1883